Ed's NAUGTIEST LIMERICKS EVER

I0187234

Singalong with Ed

Ed's

SILLIEST
NAUGHTIEST
SINGALONG
LIMERICKS

They were Naughty
once
and they still are!
ENJOY!

ISBN 978-0-9810702-0-9

NOTICE

Some of these ballads are course and vulgar. They are sung at your own risk. I take no responsibility for the outcome, the laughs, the scorn or the aggression that may arise from the use of this "Adult" material. These Ballads are taken from the worst military, rugby, bar and back room songs written.

This song book is provided for private use and is a compilation of the best (worst) of my favorite songs. I compiled them for my own use and simply use CafePress to print them for me. All material has been taken from the public domain and the book is not meant for commercial use. If you happen to wander here, and want a copy, it is for your private fun and enjoyment and I do not guarantee the accuracy of the chords, words or material. I do guarantee, however, that these songs when sung in the right place (whatever that is) will give you fun and laughs.

Ed Rychkun

www.edrychkun.com

WHAT'S A LIMERICK?

Besides being a city in Ireland, Limerick is a five-line poem with a strict form, originally popularized in English by Edward Lear. Limericks are frequently witty or funny, and sometimes obscene with humorous intent. Here is an example of a limerick with the chords:

C   G7
There was a young lady named Lou
                                  C
who said as the parson withdrew:
    C
"Now the Vicar is quicker,
        F
And thicker, and slicker,
    G7   C
And two inches longer than you".

Then there is the chorus:

C   G7
That was a cute little rhyme,
G7   G7
Sing us another one, just like the other one,
                          C
Sing us another one do -- oo

Then the next verse:

There was a young man from Nantucket
Whose cock was so long he could suck it
And he said with a grin
As he wiped off his chin--

"If my ear was a cunt I could fuck it."[1]

Here's another chorus that may be more appropriate:

> **That was a horrible rhyme,**
> **Sing us another one, just like the other one,**
> **Sing us another one do.**

And the next verse

> **Here's to old king Montazuma**
> **For fun he buggered a puma**
> **The puma one day**
> **Bit both balls away**
> **An example of animal humor.**

Here's a chorus that also works

> **That was a funny old rhyme, here comes another verse,**
> **Worse than the other verse, sing us another one do.**
> **Chorus :**

And so on...

> **There was a young man from Samoa**
> **Who had just one inch, and no more**
> **It was all right for keyholes**
> **And little girl's pee-holes**
> **but not worth a damn to a whore.**

Pick your chorus and the next singer.

This form of "poetry" referred to as Limerick poems have received a lot of bad press and dismissed as not having a rightful place amongst what is seen as 'cultivated poetry'. This is because the content of many limericks is often of a bawdy and humorous nature, and a Limerick as a poetry form is by nature simple and short - limericks only have five lines. But limericks have a somewhat dubious history that has contributed to the critic's attitudes.

Variants of the this form of poetry can be traced back to the fourteenth century English history. Limericks were used in Nursery Rhymes and other poems for children. But as limericks were short, relatively easy to compose and bawdy or sexual in nature they were often repeated by beggars or the working classes in the British pubs and taverns of the fifteenth, sixteenth and seventh centuries. The poets who created these limericks were therefore often drunkards! So Limericks got the rap as being dirty – and in many cases, rightly so.

The word derives from the Irish town of Limerick. Apparently a pub song or tavern chorus based on the refrain "Will you come up to Limerick?" where, of course, such bawdy songs or 'Limericks' were sung. In structure, Limericks consist of five anapaestic lines. Lines 1, 2, and 5 of Limericks have seven to ten syllables and rhyme with one another. Lines 3 and 4 of Limericks have five to seven syllables and also rhyme with each other. For example:

> A   **There was a young man named Perkin**
> A   **who was furtively jerking his gerkin**
> B   **His wife's face grew red**
> B   **As to him she said**
> A   **Perkin you're shirkin your perkin**

As above, a limerick has five lines, with three metrical feet (like groups of words i.e. there was... a young man... named Perkin) in the first, second, and fifth lines and two metrical feet in the third and fourth lines. (His wife's face... grew red). A variety of types of metrical foot can be used, but the most typical are the amphibrach (a stressed syllable between two unstressed syllables) and the anapaest (two unstressed syllables followed by a stressed syllable).[1] The rhyme scheme is usually AABBA.

The first line of a limerick traditionally introduces a person and a place, with the place appearing at the end of the first line and therefore establishing the rhyme scheme for the second and fifth lines. In early limericks, the last line was often essentially a repeat of the first line, although this is no longer customary.

Within the genre, ordinary speech stress is often distorted in the first line, and may be regarded as a feature of the form: "There WAS a young MAN from the COAST;" "There ONCE was a GIRL from DeTROIT Exploitation of geographical names, especially exotic ones, is also common, and has been seen as invoking memories of geography lessons in order to subvert the decorum taught in the schoolroom; One finds that the exchange of limericks is almost exclusive to comparatively well-educated males (women figuring in limericks almost exclusively as "villains or victims"). The most prized limericks incorporate a kind of twist, which may be revealed in the final line, or may lie in the way the rhymes are often intentionally tortured, or both. Many limericks additionally show some form of internal rhyme, alliteration or assonance, or some element of wordplay. Some examples exploit the strict form of the limerick to lead the listener into expecting a particular conclusion, particularly one that would be obscene or shocking, and then derive humour from cunningly avoiding the expected words. Well, that's what the objective is-

But one has to admit the content of Limericks can often verge on the indecent, the dirty, chauavanistic, or even the totally obscene, but they make people laugh! And perhaps it is this laughability that transcends the crude? Limericks are easy to remember! Limericks are short and no great talent is necessary to compose one - Limericks are a form of poetry that everyone feels happy to try (especially when inebriated!). Limericks as a form of poetry has survived the test of time dating back for centuries! And while the poetic and literary skills of Shakespeare are not necessary for the composition of a limerick the great Bard himself did in fact write limericks which can be found in two of his greatest plays - Othello and King Lear.

Edward Lear's Book of Nonsense included the poetry form of Limericks. His work with limericks were, however, not in any way indecent and this particular book proved to be extremely popular in the nineteenth century and this was contributed to by the humorous magazine Punch which started printing examples of limericks leading to a craze by its readers. The first edition of Edward Lear's Book of Nonsense was published by Thomas McLean on 10th February 1846. There were altogether seventy-two limericks in two volumes which sold at 3s 6d each. These limericks have proven to be extremely popular with children.

Some of the original Limericks by Edward Lear from A Book of Nonsense are included in the next section.

LIMERICKS BY EDWARD LEAR
1812-1888

There was an Old Man with a beard,
Who said, 'It is just as I feared!
Two Owls and a Hen,
Four Larks and a Wren,
Have all built their nests in my beard!'

There was an Old Man of Kilkenny,
Who never had more than a penny;
He spent all that money,
In onions and honey,
That wayward Old Man of Kilkenny.

There was an Old Man of Vienna,
Who lived upon Tincture of Senna;
When that did not agree,
He took Camomile Tea,
That nasty Old Man of Vienna.

There was a Young Lady whose eyes,
Were unique as to colour and size;
When she opened them wide,
People all turned aside,
And started away in surprise.

There was an Old Man who supposed,
That the street door was partially closed;
But some very large rats,
Ate his coats and his hats,
While that futile old gentleman dozed.

There was an Old Man of Columbia,
Who was thirsty, and called out for some beer;
But they brought it quite hot,
In a small copper pot,
Which disgusted that man of Columbia.

There was an Old Man of the West,
Who wore a pale plum-coloured vest;
When they said, 'Does it fit?'
He replied, 'Not a bit!'
That uneasy Old Man of the West.

There was on Old Man of the Isles,
Whose face was pervaded with smiles;
He sung high dum diddle,
And played on the fiddle,
That amiable Man of the Isles.

There was an Old Person of Hurst,
Who drank when he was not athirst;
When they said, 'You'll grw fatter,'
He answered, 'What matter?'
That globular Person of Hurst.

There was an Old Man with a gong,
Who bumped at it all day long;
But they called out, 'O law!
You're a horrid old bore!'
So they smashed that Old Man with a gong.

There was a Young Person of Smyrna,
Whose Grandmother threatened to burn her;
But she seized on the cat,
And said, 'Granny, burn that!
You incongruous Old Woman of Smyrna!'

There was an Old Man on a hill,
Who seldom, if ever, stood still;
He ran up and down,
In his Grandmother's gown,
Which adorned that Old Man on a hill.

There was a Young Lady whose bonnet,
Came untied when the birds sate upon it;
But she said: 'I don't care!

All the birds in the air
Are welcome to sit on my bonnet!'

There was a Young Lady of Ryde,
Whose shoe-strings were seldom untied.
She purchased some clogs,
And some small spotted dogs,
And frequently walked about Ryde.

There was an Old Man of Moldavia,
Who had the most curious behaviour;
For while he was able,
He slept on a table.
That funny Old Man of Moldavia.

There was a Young Lady of Portugal,
Whose ideas were excessively nautical:
She climbed up a tree,
To examine the sea,
But declared she would never leave Portugal.

There was an Old Person of Dover,
Who rushed through a field of blue Clover;
But some very large bees,
Stung his nose and his knees,
So he very soon went back to Dover.

There was an Old Person of Basing,
Whose presence of mind was amazing;
He purchased a steed,
Which he rode at full speed,
And escaped from the people of Basing.

The was a Young Lady of Bute,
Who played on a silver-gilt flute;
She played several jigs,
To her uncle's white pigs,
That amusing Young Lady of Bute.

There was an Old Man in a tree,
Who was horribly bored by a Bee;
When they said, 'Does it buzz?'
He replied, 'Yes, it does!'
'It's a regular brute of a Bee!'

There was an Old Man with a flute,
A sarpint ran into his boot;
But he played day and night,
Till the sarpint took flight,
And avoided that man with a flute.

There was an Old Person whose habits,
Induced him to feed upon rabbits;
When he'd eaten eighteen,
He turned perfectly green,
Upon which he relinquished those habits.

There was an Old Man of the Wrekin
Whose shoes made a horrible creaking
But they said, 'Tell us whether,
Your shoes are of leather,
Or of what, you Old Man of the Wrekin?'

There was a Young Lady of Dorking,
Who bought a large bonnet for walking;
But its colour and size,
So bedazzled her eyes,
That she very soon went back to Dorking.

There was an Old Person of Buda,
Whose conduct grew ruder and ruder;
Till at last, with a hammer,
They silenced his clamour,
By smashing that Person of Buda.

There was a Young Lady of Norway,
Who casually sat on a doorway;
When the door squeezed her flat,

She exclaimed, 'What of that?'
This courageous Young Lady of Norway.

There was a Young Person of Crete,
Whose toilette was far from complete;
She dressed in a sack,
Spickle-speckled with black,
That ombliferous person of Crete.

There was an Old Lady of Chertsey,
Who made a remarkable curtsey;
She twirled round and round,
Till she sunk underground,
Which distressed all the people of Chertsey.

There was an Old Man in a tree,
Who was horribly bored by a Bee;
When they said, 'Does it buzz?'
He replied, 'Yes, it does!'
'It's a regular brute of a Bee!'

There was an Old Person of Chili,
Whose conduct was painful and silly,
He sate on the stairs,
Eating apples and pears,
That imprudent Old Person of Chili.

There was a Young Lady whose chin,
Resembled the point of a pin;
So she had it made sharp,
And purchased a harp,
And played several tunes with her chin.

There was an Old Man of Madras,
Who rode on a cream-coloured ass;
But the length of its ears,
So promoted his fears,
That it killed that Old Man of Madras.

There was an Old Man of Peru,
Who never knew what he should do;
So he tore off his hair,
And behaved like a bear,
That intrinsic Old Man of Peru.

There was an Old Man in a boat,
Who said, 'I'm afloat, I'm afloat!'
When they said, 'No! you ain't!'
He was ready to faint,
That unhappy Old Man in a boat.

There was an Old Man with a nose,
Who said, 'If you choose to suppose,
That my nose is too long,
You are certainly wrong!'
That remarkable Man with a nose.

There was an Old Person of Ischia,
Whose conduct grew friskier and friskier;
He dance hornpipes and jigs,
And ate thousands of figs,
That lively Old Person of Ischia.

There was an Old Man of Marseilles,
Whose daughters wore bottle-green veils;
They caught several Fish,
Which they put in a dish,
And sent to their Pa' at Marseilles.

There was an Old Person of Cadiz,
Who was always polite to all ladies;
But in handing his daughter,
He fell into the water,
Which drowned that Old Person of Cadiz.

There was an old man of Tobago,
Who lived on rice, gruel and sago
Till, much to his bliss,

His physician said this -
To a leg, sir, of mutton you may go.

There was a Young Lady in White,
Who looked out at the depths of the Night;
But the birds of the air
Filled her heart with despair,
And oppressed that Young Lady in White.

There was a Young Lady of Lucca,
Whose lovers completely forsook her;
She ran up a tree
And said, 'Fiddle-de-dee!'
Which embarrassed the people of Lucca.

There was a Young Lady of Parma,
Whose conduct grew calmer and calmer;
When they said, 'Are you dumb?
She merely said, 'Hum!'
That provoking Young Lady of Parma.

There was a Young Lady of Tyre,
Who swept the loud chords of a lyre;
At the sound of each sweep
She enraptured the deep,
And enchanted the city of Tyre.

There was a Young Person of Smyrna,
Whose grandmother threatened to burn her;
But she seized on the cat,
And said, 'Granny, burn that!
You incongruous old woman of Smyrna!'

There was a young person whose history
Was always considered a mystery.
She sate in a ditch,
Although no one knew which,
And composed a small treatise on history.

There was an Old Lady of Chertsey,
Who made a remarkable curtsey;
She twirled round and round,
Till she sunk underground,
Which distressed all the people of Chertsey.

There was an old Lady of Winchelsea,
Who said, 'If you needle or pin shall see
On the floor of my room,
Sweep it up with the broom!'
- That exhaustive old Lady of Winchelsea!

There was an Old Man in a boat,
Who said, 'I'm afloat! I'm afloat!'
When they said, 'No! you aint!'
He was ready to faint,
That unhappy Old Man in a boat.

There was an Old Man in a tree,
Who was horribly bored by a bee.
When they said, 'Does it buzz?'
He replied, 'Yes, it does!
It's a regular brute of a bee!'

There was an Old Man in a Tree,
Whose Whiskers were lovely to see;
But the Birds of the Air
Pluck'd them perfectly bare
To make themselves Nests in that Tree.

There was an Old Man of Thermopylae,
Who never did anything properly;
But they said, 'If you choose
To boil Eggs in your Shoes,
You shall never remain in Thermopylae.'

There was an Old Man of Toulouse
Who purchased a new pair of shoes.
When they asked, 'Are they pleasant?' -

He said, 'Not at present!'
That turbid old man of Toulouse.

There was an Old Man of Cape Horn,
Who wished he had never been born;
So he sat on a chair
Till he died of despair,
That dolorous Man of Cape Horn.

There was an Old Man of Hong Kong,
Who never did anything wrong.
He lay on his back,
With his head in a sack,
That innocuous Old Man of Hong Kong.

There was an Old Man on the Border,
Who lived in the utmost disorder;
He danced with the Cat,
And made Tea in his Hat,
Which vexed all the folks on the Border.

There was an Old Man who said, 'Hush!
I perceive a young bird in this bush.!'
When they said, 'Is it small?'
He replied, 'Not at all!
It is four times as big as the bush!'

There was an Old Man who, when little,
Fell casually into a Kettle;
But, growing too stout,
He could never get out,
So he passed all his life in that Kettle.

There was an old man whose despair
Induced him to purchase a hare:
Whereon one fine day,
He rode wholly away,
Which partly assuaged his despair.

There was an Old Man with a beard,
Who said 'It is just as I feared! -
Two Owls and a Hen,
Four Larks and a Wren,
Have all built their nests in my beard!'

There was an Old Man with a beard,
Who sat on a horse when he reared;
But they said, 'Never mind!
You will fall off behind,
You propitious Old Man with a beard!'

There was an Old Person in Black,
A Grasshopper jumped on his back;
When it chirped in his ear,
He was smitten with fear,
That helpless Old Person in Black.

There was an Old Person in Gray,
Whose feelings were tinged with disman;
She purchased two Parrots,
And fed them with Carrots,
Which pleased that Old Person in Gray.

There was an Old Person of Basing,
Whose presence of mind was amazing;
He purchased a steed,
Which he rode at full speed,
And escaped from the people of Basing.

There was an Old Person of Fife,
Who was greatly disgusted with life;
They sang him a ballad,
And fed him on Salad,
Which cured that Old Person of Fife.

There was an Old Person of Gretna,
Who rushed down the crater of Etna;
When they said, 'Is it hot?'

He replied, 'No, it's not!'
That mendacious Old Person of Gretna.

There was an Old Person of Putney,
Whose food was roast spiders and chutney,
Which he took with his tea
Within sight of the sea,
That romantic Old Person of Putney.

There was an Old Person of Slough,
Who danced at the end of a Bough;
But they said, 'If you sneeze,
You might damage the trees,
You imprudent Old Person of Slough.

There was an Old Person of Ware
Who rode on the back of a Bear;
When they ask'd, 'Does it trot?'
He said, 'Certainly not!
He's a Moppsikon Floppsikon Bear!'

There was an Old Person of Wick,
Who said, 'Tick-a-Tick, Tick-a-Tick;
Chickabee, Chickabaw.'
And he said nothing more,
That laconic Old Person of Wick.

SOME TRADITIONAL LIMERICKS

There once was a man from Rangoon,
Whose farts could be heard to the moon.
When you'd least expect 'em,
They'd explode from his rectum,
With the force of a raging typhoon.

The jolly old Bishop of Birmingham,
He buggered 3 maids while confirming 'em,
As they knelt seeking God,
He excited his rod,
And pumped his episcopal sperm in'em.

There once was a man named Skinner,
Who took a young lady to dinner,
At quarter past ten it was in her,
Dinner, not Skinner,
Skinner was in her before dinner.

There once was a man from Boston,
Who drove around in an Austin,
There was room for his ass,
And a gallon of gas,
But his balls hung out and he lost 'em.

Who swallowed a package of seeds,
Great tufts of grass,
Sprouted out of his ass,
And his balls were covered with weeds.

Aye, yi, yi, yi
Rodriguez, the Mexican pervert.
He ate out his mother
And cornholed his brother,
And waltzed me around by my willy.

There once was a lady from Peru,
Who filled her vagina with glue,

She said with a grin,
If they'll pay to get in,
They'll pay to get out of it too.

There was a couple named Kelly,
Who were stuck belly to belly,
Because of their haste,
They used library past,
Instead of petroleum jelly.

There was a young lady of Cheam,
Who crept into the vestry unseen,
She pulled down her knickers,
Likewise the vicar's,
And said, "How about it, old bean'?"

There once was a man from Racine,
Who built a big fucking machine,
Concave or convex,
It would fuck any sex,
Oh but what a bastard to clean.

There was a young German named Ringer
Who was screwing an opera singer,
Said he with a grin,
"Well, I've sure got it in!"
Said she, "It ain't your finger?"

There was a young lady named Hitchin,
Scratching her crotch in the kitchen,
Her mother said, "Rose,
It's the crabs I suppose?"
She said, "Yes and the buggers are itchin."

There was a young man of St. James,
Who indulged in the jolliest games,
He lighted the rim,
Of his grandmother's quim,
And made her piss through the flames.

There was a young woman named Wheeli
Who professed of no sexual feeling,
Until a cynic named Boris,
Nibbled at her clitoris,
Wheeling was scraped from the ceiling.

A hermit who had an oasis,
Thought it the best of all places,
He could pray and be calm,
'Neath a pleasant date palm,
While the lice on his penis ran races.

There was a young lady of Exeter,
So pretty, men craned their necks at her,
One went so far,
As to wave from his car,
The distinguishing mark of his sex at her.

There once was a man from Nantuckett,
With a cock so long he could suck it,
He said with a grin,
As he wiped off his chin,
"If my ear was a cunt I could fuck it."

Female apes were afraid of King Kong,
Since his wanger was exceedingly long,
Until a friendly giraffe,
Ate his yard and a half,
And ecstatically burst into song.

There was a young lady from Trent,
Who said she knew what it meant,
When he asked her to dine,
Private room, lots of wine,
She knew, she knew, but she went.

There once was a man from Madras,
Who balls were made from brass,

In windy Wea ther
They swung together,
And lightening shot out his ass.

In the Garden of Eden lay Adam,
Complacently stroking his madam,
For he knew in his mirth,
That on all of the earth,
There were only two balls and he had 'em.

A fellow whose surname was Hunt,
Trained his prick to do a stunt,
This versatile spout,
Could be turned inside out,
like a glove and be used as a cunt.

There once was a man from Kajowels,
Whose diet consisted of bowels,
When he couldn't get this,
He drank prostitute piss,
And scrapings from sanitary towels.

There was a woman from the Azores,
Whose body was covered with sores,
All the dogs in the street,
Would lick the green meat,
That hung down from her drawers.

That poor young fellow from Kent,
Whose cock was so exceedingly bent,
To save himself the trouble,
He ut it in double,
And instead of coming he went.

There once was a man named Bruno,
About tucking sheep he do know,
Lambs are fine,
And rams are divine,
But Lamas are numero uno.

There was a young lady named Hilda,
Who went for a walk with a builder,
He knew that he could,
And he should, and he would,
So he did, and he damn near killed her.

A young man with passions quite gingery,
Tore a hole in his Sister's best lingerie,
He slapped her behind,
And made up his mind,
To add incest to insult and injury.

There was a young lady of Crewe,
Whose cherry a chap had got through,
Which she told to her mother,
Who fixed her another,
Out of rubber, red ink, and glue.

When a lecherous priest at Leeds,
Was discovered, one day in the weeds,
Astride a young nun,
He said, "Christ this is fun,
Far better than fondling one's beads."

There was a young lady of Twickerham,
Who regretted men had no prick in 'em,
On her knees everyday,
To her God she would pray,
To lengthen, strengthen, and thicken 'em.

There was a young girl named McCall,
Whose cunt was exceedingly small,
But the size of her anus,
Was something quite heinous,
It could hold seven cocks and one ball.

There was a young parson named Binns,
Who talked about women and things,

But his secret desire,
Was a boy in the choir,
With a bottom like jelly on springs.

There was a young man of high station,
Who was found by a pious relation,
Making love in a ditch,
To I won't say a bitch,
But a woman of no reputation.

There was a young girl of Detroit,
Who at fucking was very adroit,
She could squeeze her vagina,
To a pinpoint or finer,
Or open it out like a quoit.

There was a young maid from Mobile,
Whose cunt was made of blue steel,
She got her thrills,
From pneumatic drills,
And off-centered emery wheels.

There was a young nun from Siberia,
Endowed with a virgin interior,
Until an old monk,
Jumped into her bunk,
And now she's the Mother Superior.

There was a young Scot from Delray,
Who buggered his father one day,
Saying, "I like it rather,
To stuff it up father,
He's clean and nothing's to pay."

There was a young plumber of Lea,
Who was plumbing a girl by the sea,
She said, "Stop your plumbing,
There's somebody coming!" -
Said he, still plumbing, "It's me."

There was an old man of Dundee,
Who came home as drunk as could be,
He wound up the clock,
With the end of his cock,
And buggered his wife with the key.

There was a young man from Lynn,
Whose cock was the size of a pin,
Said his girl with a laugh,
As she fondled his shaft,
"This won't be much of a sin."

An elderly pervert in Nice,
Who was long past wanting a piece,
Would jack-off his hogs,
His cows and his dogs,
Till his parrot called the police.

There was a young man from Cape Horn,
Who wished he had never been born,
And he wouldn't have been,
Had his father seen,
That the end of his rubber was torn.

The last time I dined with the King,
He did quite an unkingly thing,
While up on the throne,
He pulled out his bone,
And said, "If I play, will you sing?"

A comely young widow of Ransom,
Was ravished three times in a hansom,
When she cried out for more,
A voice from the floor,
Said, "Lady, I'm Simpson, not Sampson."

There once was a skater named Yeats,
Who attempted the splits while on skates,

But he fell on his cutlass,
Which rendered him nutless,
And now he is useless on dates.

From the depths of a crypt at St. Ciles,
Came a scream that resounded for miles,
Said the bishop, "Good gracious,
Has Father Ignatious
Forgotten the vicar has piles?"

There was an old Duke of Rockingham,
Who wrote a book on cunts and tucking 'em,
But a dirty old Turk,
Wrote a much better work,
On tits and 12 ways of sucking 'em.

There was a young girl from Yorkshire,
Who succumbed to her lover's desire,
She said, "Oh John, it's a sin,
But now that it's in,
Would you shove it a few inches higher?"

There was a young man from Brighton,
Who thought he had found a tight one,
He said, "Oh my love,
It fits like a glove."
She said, "But it's not in the right one."

There was a hermit from Behave,
Who kept a dead whore in his cave,
She only had one tit,
And smelled like shit,
But think of the money he saved.

There was a man of New Treaver,
Who had intercourse with a beaver,
The result of his screw,
Was a birchbark canoe,
Three ducks and an Irish retriever.

The gay young Duke of Buckingham,
Stood on the bridge at Rockingham,
Watching the stunts,
Of the cunts midst the grunts,
And all of the pricks fucking 'em.

There was a student of Trinity,
Who popped his sister's virginity,
Buggered his brother,
Had twins by his mother,
And took double honor in Divinity.

There once was a young Dr. Zuck,
In his ears her nipples got stuck,
With his thumb up her bum,
He could hear himself come,
Thus inventing the telephone tick.

The three old witches of Kent,
Took a man into a tent,
The three dirty bitches,
They pulled down his britches,
And jumped on his cock til it bent.

There was a young man named Pete,
Who was a bit indiscreet,
He pulled on his wong,
Until it grew very long,
And dragged down a two lane street.

There was a young man from Stroud,
Who was screwing a girl in a crowd,
A man up in front,
Said, "Hmmm, I smell cunt."
Just like that, not very loud.

There was a young lawyer named Springer,
Got his testicles caught in the wringer,

He hollered with pain
As they went down the drain,
"From now on I'll just use my finger."

Coitus upon a cadaver,
Is the ultimate way you can have 'er,
Her inanimate state,
Means a man needn't wait,
And eliminates all the palaver.

There once was a chick named Alice,
Who used a dynamite stick for a phallus,
When she got hot,
It finally went pop,
And they found her tits outside of Dallas.

There once was a girl from Nantuckett,
Who went to France in a bucket,
When she got there,
They asked for her fare,
She lifted up her dress and said fuck it.

I once knew a man named Magruder,
Who met a nude and he wooed her,
The nude thought it crude,
To be wooed in the nude,
But Magruder was shrewder and screwed her

There was a young girl from France,
Who jumped on a bus in a trance,
Six passengers fucked her,
Besides the conductor,
And the driver shot twice in his pants.

A pansy by the name of Bloom,
Took a lesbian up to his room,
They talked the whole night,
As to who had the right,
To do what, with which, and to whom.

There was a young man named Mirkin,
Who kept on jerkin' his gherkin,
Said his wife to Mirkin,
"Your duty you're shirkin',
That gherkin's for firkin', not jerkin'."

A young man whose sight was myopic,
Thought sex an incredible topic,
So poor were his eyes,
That despite its great size,
His prick appeared microscopic.

I once knew a girl named Delores,
Who had a six-inch clitoris,
While singing a chorus,
Her voice was so hoarse,
I checked her ID and it said Boris.

I once knew a man from LaGrange,
His mind was completely deranged,
In playgrounds he hung,
Looking at ten year old bun,
This was his home on the range.

There was a girl from Cape Cod,
Who thought babies were from God,
But 'twas not the Almighty,
Who hiked up her nightie,
'Twas Roger, the lodger, by God.

There once was a man named Hans,
Who planted an acre of cunts,
When in the fall,
They came up pubic hairs and all,
Hans ate cunts for months.

There was a young lady named Duff,
With a lively, luxuriant muff,

In his haste to get in her,
One eager beginner,
Lost both his balls in the rough.

There was a young man of Kildare,
Fucking a girl on the stairs,
The bannister broke,
But he doubled his stroke,
And finished her off in midair.

I once knew a man named Peese,
It was said he was quite a tease,
But along came Jan,
Who spread him some ham,
And together they made some cheese.

There was a young Turkish cadet,
And this is the damnedest one yet,
His tool was so long,
And incredibly strong,
He could bugger six Greeks en brochette

There was a dentist Malone,
Who fondled a girl patient alone,
But in his depravity,
He filled the wrong cavity,
And my how his practice has grown.

There once was a man named O'Dool,
Who had an enormous tool,
He'd use it to plow,
Or didle a cow,
Or as a cue stick at pool.

There once was a man from Shirue,
Who had warts all over his root,
He put acid on these,
And now when he pees,
He fingers his dick like a flute.

There was a soldier from Kildare,
Who fondled a girl in his chair,
At the sixty-third stroke,
The chair done broke,
And his gun went off in the air.

There was a young lady from Itching,
Sat scratching her crutch in the kitchen,
Her Mother said, ``Rose, it's pox I suppose,''
She said, ``Bollocks, get on with your knitting.''

There was a young fella named Dave,
Who found a dead whore in a cave,
It took him some pluck to have a cold fuck,
But look at the money he saved.

There was a young girl from Australia,
Whose cunt did smell like a dahlia,
At 5p a smell it went very well,
At 10p a lick was a failure.

There was a young girl from Cape Cod,
Who thought that all babes came from God,
It wasn't the Almighty who lifted her nighty,
It was Roger the lodger the sod.

There was a young lady from Gannon,
Who had an affair with the Reverend Buchanan,
She said with a grin, as he slipped it right in,
With those balls you should be a Cannon.

There was a young man from Bengal,
Who had a hexagonal ball,
Its molecular weight was his prick times eight,
And twice the square root of fuck all.

There was a young maid from Mobile,
Whose cunt was made of blue steel,

She got her thrills from pneumatic drills,
And off-centred emery wheels.

There was a young nun from Siberia,
Endowed with a virgin interior,
Until an old monk jumped into her bunk,
And now she's the Mother Superior.

There was a young Scot from Delray,
Who buggered his father one day,
Saying I like it rather, to stuff it up father,
He's clean and there's nothing to pay.

There was a young plumber of Lea,
Who was plumbing a girl by the sea,
She said, ``Stop your plumbing, there's somebody coming.'
Said the Plumber still plumbing, ``It's me !"

The gay young Duke of Buckingham,
Stood on the bridge at Rockingham,
Watching the stunts of the cunts on the punts,
And the tricks of the pricks that were stuffing 'em.

There was a young girl from Azores,
Whose cunt was covered in sores,
All the dogs in the street, would lick the green meat,
That hung in festoons from her drawers.

There was a young sailor from Brighton,
Who remarked to his girl, "You're a tight one."
She replied, "Pon my soul, you're in the wrong hole,
There's plenty of room in the right one."

There was a young fellow named Charteris,
Put his hand where his young lady's garter is,
She said, "I don't mind, and up higher you'll find,
The place where my fucker and farter is."

There were three ladies of Huxham,

And whenever we meets 'em, we fucks 'em,
And when that game grows stale, we sits on the rail,
And pulls out our pricks and they sucks 'em.

There was a young man of Ostend,
Whose wife caught him fucking her friend,
"It's no use my duck, interrupting our fuck,
For I'm damned if I'll draw till I spend."

There was a young German named Ringer,
Who was screwing an opera singer,
He said with a grin, "Well I've sure shoved it in!"
Said she, "You mean that ain't your finger."

There once was a dentist named Stone,
Who saw all his patients alone,
In a fit of depravity, he filled the wrong cavity,
And my, how his practice has grown.

A sailor who slept in the sun,
Woke to find his fly buttons undone,
He remarked with a smile, "Fuck me, a sundial,
And now it's a quarter to one."

There was a young fellow of Harrow,
Whose john was the size of a marrow,
He said to his tart, "How's this for a start ?
My balls are outside in a barrow."

There was a young lady named Mable,
Who liked to sprawl out on the table,
Then cry to her man, "Stuff in all you can,
Get your bollocks in to, if you're able."

There was a young lass of Blackheath,
Who frigged an old man with her teeth,
She complained that he stunk, not so much from the spunk,
But his arsehole was just underneath.

There was a young person of Kent,
Who was famous wherever he went,
All the way through a fuck, he would quack like a duck,
And he crowed like a cock when he spent.

A parson who lived near Camborne,
Looked down on all women with scorn,
E'en a boy's fat, white bum,
could not make him come,
But an old man's piles gave him the horn.

A mortician who practiced in Fife,
Made love to the corpse of his wife,
"How could I know, Judge, she was cold, did not budge,
Just the same as she'd acted in life."

A Sultan of old Istanbul,
Had a varicose vein on his tool,
This evoked joyous grunts, from his harem of cunts,
But his boys suffered pain at the stool.

There was an old man of Kentucky,
Said to his old woman, "Oi'll fuck 'ee."
She replied, "Now you wunt, come anigh my old cunt,
For your prick is all stinking and mucky."

There was a young mate of a lugger,
Who took out a girl just to hug her,
"I've my monthlies," she said,
 "and a cold in the head,
But my bowels work well.....Do you bugger ?"

There was a young man of Bengal,
Who went to a fancy dress ball,
Just for a stunt, he dressed up as a cunt,
And was fucked by a dog in the hall.

There was a young man named McBride,
Who could fart whenever he tried,

In a contest he blew, two thousand and two,
Then shit and was disqualified.

There was a young lady from Crewe,
Who filled her vagina with glue,
She said with a grin, "If they pay to get in,
They'll pay to get out of it too."

A notorious whore named Miss Hearst,
In the weakness of men is well versed,
Reads the sign o'er the head, of her well rumpled bed,
"The customer always comes first."

There was a young lady of Newcastle,
Who wrapped up a turd in a parcel,
And sent it to a relation, with this invitation,
"It has just come out hot from my arsehole."

My old woman would wipe off her bum,
Of the clinkers that thereunto hung,
She would singe off the hair, that had sprouted down there,
And would lick her twat clean with her tongue.

There was a young man of Jaipur,
Whose cock was shot off in the war,
So he painted the front to resemble a cunt,
And set himself up as a whore.

There was an old girl of Silesia,
Who said, "As my cunt doesn't please ya,
You might as well come up my old slimy bum,
But be careful my tapeworm don't seize ya."

There was a young man from Poole,
Who found a red ring round his tool,
He ran to the clinic, but the doctor, a cynic,
Said, "That's only lipstick, you fool."

There was a young fellow named Bill,

Who took an atomic pill,
His navel corroded, his arsehole exploded,
And they found his burnt nuts in Brazil.

There was a young man of Canute,
Who was troubled by warts on his root,
He put acid on these, and now when he pees,
He can finger his root like a flute.

There was an old person of Gosham,
Who took out his bollocks to wash 'em,
His wife said, "Now Jack, if you don't put them back,
I'll step on your scrotum and squash 'em."

Did you hear about young Henry Lockett ?
He was blown down the street by a rocket,
The force of the blast blew his balls up his arse,
And his pecker was found in his pocket.

There was a young lady of Tring,
Who sat by the fire to sing,
A piece of charcoal, flew up her arsehole,
And burnt all the hair off her quim.

There was a young man of Bombay,
Who fashioned a cunt out of clay,
But the heat of his prick, turned it into a brick,
And chafed all his foreskin away.

A certain young fellow named Dick,
Liked to feel a girl's hand on his prick,
He taught them to fool, with his rigid old tool,
Till the cream shot out, white and thick.

A bus-man named Abner McFuss,
Liked to suck off old men on his bus,
Then go out and sniff turds, and the arseholes of birds,
He sure was a funny old cuss.

There was a young man named Morell,
Who played with his prick till he fell,
When to get up he started, he suddenly farted,
And fell down again from the smell.

There once was a lady called Annie,
Who had fleas, lice and crabs up her fanny,
To get up her flue was like touring the zoo,
There were wild beasts in each nook and cranny.

An insatiable nymph from Penzance,
Travelled by bus to south Hants,
Five others fucked her, besides the conductor,
And the driver came twice in his pants.

There was a young man from Nantucket,
Whose cock was so long he could suck it,
He said with a grin as he wiped off his chin,
"If my ear was a cunt, I could fuck it."

There was a young girl named McCall,
Whose cunt was exceedingly small,
But the size of her anus was something quite heinous,
It could hold seven pricks and one ball.

There was a young man of St James,
Who indulged in the jolliest games,
He lighted the rim of his grandmother's quim,
And laughed as she pissed through the flames.

There was a young man named Hentzel,
Who had a terrific long pencil,
He went through an actress, two sheets and a mattress,
And shattered the family utensil.

There once was a rabbi named Keith,
Who circumcised men with his teeth,
It was not for the treasure, nor sexual pleasure,
But to get to the cheese underneath.

There was a young man named Adair,
Who was fucking a girl on the stair,
The banister broke, and by doubling his stroke,
He finished her off in mid air.

There was a young lady from Munich,
Who was ravished one night by a eunuch,
At the height of her passion he slipped her a ration,
From a squirt gun concealed in his tunic.

A policeman from near Clapham junction,
Had a penis that just wouldn't function,
For the rest of his life he misled his wife,
With some snot on the end of his truncheon.

MORE MODERN DAY LIMERICKS

There was an Old Man of Quebec,
A beetle ran over his neck;
But he cried, 'With a needle,
I'll slay you, O beadle!'
That angry Old Man of Quebec.

The fabulous Wizard of Oz
Retired from business becoz
What with up-to-date science,
To most of his clients,
He wasn't the Wizard he woz.

There was a young woman named Bright
Whose speed was much faster than light.
She set out one day
In a relative way,
And returned on the previous night.

A flea and a fly in a flue
Were imprisoned, so what could they do?
Said the fly, "Let us flee!"
"Let us fly," said the flea,
So they flew through a flaw in the flue.

There once was an Italian girl named Francotti
Who stopped every morning for biscotti,
She loved them with Cappucino,
And sometimes with a glass of vino,
The biscotti with cappucino from Kieto!

A wonderful bird is the pelican,
His bill can hold more than his belican.
He can take I his beak
Food enough for a week;
But I'm damned if I see how the helican.

A tutor who tooted a flute,
Tried to teach two tooters to toot.
Said the two to the tutor,
"Is it harder to toot, or
To tutor two tutors to toot?"

There was a young lady named Rose
Who had a large wart on her nose.
When she had it removed
Her appearance improved,
But her glasses slipped down to her toes.

God's plan made a hopeful beginning,
But Man spoilt his chances by sinning;
We trust that the story
Will end in great glory,
But at present the other side's winning.

I once knew a guy named Dracula,
Who never used a spatula,
He just dug in his teeth,
And sucked out a plum,
And said, "How the hell did that get in there?"

I went with the Duchess to tea,
Her manners were shocking to see;
Her rumblings abdominal
Were simply phenomenal,
And everyone thought it was me.

There was an old man called Keith
Who mislaid his pair of false teeth -
Laid them on a chair,
Forgot they were there,
Sat down and was bitten underneath.

There once was a girl named Irene,
Who never dressed up for Halloween,
For it was said everyday,

She looked like dead anyway,
So keep your tradition on Halloween, Irene.

There once was a young man named Dale
Who cherished the thought of a sail.
He boarded a yacht,
But remained on his cot
Except when he hung o'er the rail!

There was a faith healer called Neal,
Who said, "Although pain isn't real,
If I sit on a pin
And it punctures my skin,
I dislike what I fancy I feel.

There was a young lady of Eton,
Whose figure had plenty of meat on.
She said, "Wed me, Jack,"
And you'll find that my back
Is a nice place to warm your cold feet on."

A glutton who came from the Rhine
When asked at what hour he would dine,
Replied, "At eleven,
At three, five and seven,
And eight and a quarter past nine.

A newspaper man named Fling
Could make "copy" from any old thing.
But the copy he wrote
Of a five dollar note
Was so good he is now in Sing Sing.

A fitful young fisher named Fisher
Once fished for some fish in a fissure,
Till a fish, with a grin,
Pulled the fisherman in--
Now they're fishing the fissure for Fisher!

Said a foolish householder of Wales,
"An odour of coal-gas prevails."
He then struck a light
And later that night
Was collected in seventeen pails.

There was an old maid of Genoa.
I blush when I think what Iowa.
She's gone to her rest,
And it's all for the best,
Otherwise I would borrow Samoa.

A rocket explorer named Wright
Once travelled much faster than light.
He set out one day
In a relative way
And returned on the previous night.

There was a composer named Liszt
Whose music no one could resist.
When he swept the keyboard
Nobody could be bored,
And now that he's gone he is missed.

A cheese that was aged and grey
Was walking and talking one day.
Said the cheese, "Kindly note
My mama was a goat
And I'm made out of curds by the whey."

There was a young man of St. Paul
Whose prick was exceedingly small.
He could bugger a bug
at the edge of a rug,
And the bug hardly felt it at all.

there was a young Girl names Dale
who put up her ass for sale.
For the sum of two bits

you could tickle her tits,
But a buck would get you real tail.

Cried the lovely young miss Molly McFee,
I'm as chaste as a woman can be!
but to judge from the guys
who swarmed her like flies,
that's spelled c-h-a-s-e-d.

There once was a man from Hong Kong,
whose penis was seven feet long.
It was bronzed when he died,
for the church of St. Clyde,
where it's now a bell clapper, Ding Dong!

There once was a young man, Horatio,
Whose girlfriend wouldn't give him fellatio,
She said, "He shouldn't pout,
'Cause he won't lick me out,
And I think one for one's a fair ratio!"
On page 2 there is a limerick that starts

I knew a lady named Claire
who had no hair down there
so she shaved her head
made a toupee and said,"
I think I'll put it down there!!!"

Bad Billy President,
you know the whitehouse resident,
he took out his tool,
now even the kids in school,
know who and what set the precident.

There once was a girl from Arden
Who gave head to a man in a garden
When he asked her, "Dear flow,
where does that stuff go?"
She replied "*gulp* beg your pardon?"

On the train, a soldier named Jack
said good-bye, and leaned out to smack
the lips of his chick
but the gtrain took-off quick
and he kissed a cow's ass down the track

Aboot wave named McGiness
brought her young career to a finis
she didnot understand
the sudden command
to break-out the Admiral's pinnace

A bearded old biker named Charlie
Took a very long ride on his Harley.
He knew that his hog
Created no smog,
'Cause he ran it on hops and malt barley.

There once was a girl from Maine
Who when fucked would experience pain
She said to her man
Listen up Dan
Get out of my rectal drain

There once was a girl called Crissy
Who had a very unusual pussy.
You could be eager to please
But it would just make you sneeze
Cuz it wasn't really a pussy, it was a cat.

There was an old Abbot most docile
Who found a remarkable fossil
He could tell from the bend
And the wart on the end
T'was the peter of Paul the Apostle.

There once was a whore named Jade
The most sought after trick in the trade

When she died she was laid
Then relaid in the shade
And no man will since part with his spade

There once was a girl on the net
When surfing she always got wet
She had miles and miles
of xxx files
Cyber sex was all she could get

there once was a silly old Widower
Who wanted to dance to the Fiddler
Though he had love in his heart
he fell for an old fart
who was the whole towns free Diddler

There once was a lady called Pam
Who took a trip on a tram
the fucking conductor
took out his constructor
and now shes wheeling a pram

there was a young professionel women from clyde,
whose surgeon cut open her hide,
he misplaced his stitches,
closed the wrong niches,
so now she does all her work on the side

There once was a lad from Nantucket
Who didn't need that damn bucket
He went to his wife
So sweet and so nice
Oh, please honey will you sucket

There once was a lad named Maurice(Morris)
Who went for a tryst with Doris
When asked how he fared
He answered with a stare
Damn! I was greatly victorious

There once lived a gravedigger named Jay
Who courted in an unusual way
The girls he would spoon
While staring up at the moon
Then he'd cover them back up with clay

There once was a gravedigger named Bert
Who was seduced by the wiles of a flirt
The two would lie prone
Until just before Dawn
Then she had to go back in the dirt

There was a young woman from winslow creek
who had her monthlies twice a week.
said a friend from woking
how provoking
no time for poking so to speak!

There was a boy who did not suck.
But he had the worst of luck.
He tripped in school,
and broke a rule,
It hurt so he said "fuck!"

There was a young lady named Brent
With a cunt of enormous extent
And so deep and so wide
The acoustics inside
Were so good you could hear when you spent.

While going down on my wife in our bed
The chandelier fell down on my head
If she didn't prefer this
That darn cunnelingis
It would have landed on my arse instead

A well hung young sailor named Bean
Could keep at it like a machine.

As he pummeled their ends,
His Society friends
All shouted out "God save the Queen!"

A lubricious young woman named Gwen
Had never learned how to say "when!"
So she did it again
And again and again
And again and again and again.

There was a lady from Kent
To a football game she went
she stood near the goal
and opened her hole
and in the football went!

There was once a boy named Hutch,
Men he liked to touch.
He did it with a rabbit,
It then became a habbit
And now he does it too much

A girl of the Enterprise crew
refused every offer to screw
Till a Vulcan named Spock
crawled under her smock
And now she is eating for two

The Enterprise girls so one hears
have chased Spock for several years
His look of disdane
has spared them great pain
For his prick is as sharp as his ears

A habit quite gross and unsavory
held the Bishop of Illi in slavery
With libidinous howls
he buggered young owls
that he kept in an underground avery

A Disturbing Tale Comes From Niger
Of A Lady, Her Donkey, And A Tiger
What Occurred In The Bush
Might Have Remained Hush Hush
But For The Ass Print On The Face Of The Tiger

There Was A Young Lady From Butte
Obsessed With A Man Of Repute
She Spent Many An Hour
Peeking In At His Shower
While Tuning The Strings Of Her Lute

There once was a man named O'Toole
Who kept his long tool on a spool
One cold night it unraveled
Into a convent it traveled
And was promptly chopped up as a Yule

There once was a fart deep within,
who thought that to stay was a sin,
So he tunneled about,
till he found his way out,
as I silently sat with a grin.

There was a young man from Zaire
Who tried to have sex with a bear
when the mean, nasty brute
took a swipe at his root
and left nothing but testes and hair!

There once was a man name of Ewing
Who thought,"why be bothered with screwing?
When its cheaper and cleaner
To finger your weiner
And besides, you can see what you're doing!"

There Once Was A Vicar Name Ben
Whose Body Was Exceedingly Thin

As He Whipped Out His Wicker
His Young Bride did Snicker
Until He Thrust In Up To His Chin

Very sex mad was Mr. Blubber
He loved to suck , fuck and bugger
But the joy of his life
Were the tits of his wife
One real and one Indian rubber

On Halloween a young girl from the Coast
Was screwed in the Park by a Ghost
At the height of Orgasm
This pale ectoplasm
Cried "I think I can feel it, almost"

There was a Stage Manager named Sherry
Who could handle all she could carry
She did "Twelve Angry Men"
Again and again
And left them all feeling quite merry.

There was an old farmer named Young
Who was quite remarkably hung.
When cleaning the stable,
his member was able
To serve as a fork for the dung.

The man in the bar was real shrewd
some may say a bit lewd
he reached out his mitts
looking for tits
but discovered the chest of a dude.

There Once Was A Gal From Vancouver
Who'd Suck On A Schlong Like A Hoover
Her Squeal Of Delight
Should Fill You With Fright
For God Alone Could Remoover

There once was a fireman named Gary,
Whose hose was nice and big, OH VERY!
His wife, she would pray
That his hose he would spray,
'Cuz that would make her merry.

Dykes or pliers said Kim,
can bend or cut wire of tin.
But when asked of which gender,
she'd prefer to "bend" her.
"Has two cuts and does not rhyme with tin"

Their once was a man named Joe
Who was an idiot,you know
He could not find
any change but a dime
So he then bought a cheap ho

There was a young man from Brazil
Who swallowed an Atom Bomb pill.
His bum back fired
His belly retired
And his willy shot over the hill

There was a young Scot named McAmiter
Who boasted excessive diameter
But it wasn't the size
That opened their eyes
Twas his rythmn, iambic pentameter

There was a young lady named Hilda
Who went on a date with a Builder
She knew that he could
And he should and he would
And he did, and it bloody nigh killed her!

There Once Was A Fellow Named Ken
Who Kept All Of His Pigs In A Pen

But A Lady From York
Ran Away With His Pork
And She Did It Again And Again

There once was a boy named nookie
Who sat on his girl friends cookie
She screamed real loud
And it made a big crowd
Then she said he won't get no more nookie

There once was a woman from Rhodesia
She would do anything to please ya
she said "it would be fine
if you fucked me from behind
I just hope my tapeworm doesn't sees ya."

There once was a man from Duluth
whose dick got shot off in his youth
He fucked with his nose
his fingers and toes
and came through a hole in his tooth

There once was a chick on the net
who decided to take a double dare bet
When she lifted her blouse
and clicked on her mouse
and found it was all soaking wet

The man from Brazil was so weird.
His friends said, 'It's perfectly clear.
He has a big dong
that he cleans all day long
by rubbing it on his long beard!'

The old drunk's dick was so wizened.
he said,'Oh my, I've been poisoned!
I had a long dong,
but now it's all gone.'
The cops said, 'Away it was pissened.'

There once was a nasty old ho
Who opened up a bakery sto
You might not find it funny
But she saved lots of money
Because she had her own yeast for the dough

There was a young fellow from Yale
Whose face was exceedingly pale.
He spent his vacation
In self-masturbation
Because of the high price of tail.

A widow whose singular vice
was to keep her late husband on ice.
Said "It's been hard since I lost him-
Ill never defrost him!
Cold comfort, but cheap at the price.

There was a young fellow named Veach
Who fell fast asleep on the beach.
His dreams of nude women
Had his proud organ brimming
and Squirting on all within reach.

There was a young man from Vancouver
Whose existence had lost its prime mover,
But its loss he supplied
with a peice of bull's hide
Two pears, and the bag from the Hoover.

Thomas Turkey was a handsome lugger
His wife was sure fond of his sugar
But on a Thanksgiving Morn
He was stuffed full of corn
By the cook, who was a bit of a Bugger

I once stopped a Turkey named Gobble
To ask why he walked with a wobble

The cook has been pressing
My arse full of Dressing
And it's give me a bit of a nobble

As a child I had a puppy named Spot
Who swam daily in our chamber pot
I must truly admit
He stank like (crap)
But I loved that puppy a lot

There once was a fellow named Jeter
Who had a skeeter alight on his peter
He said 'Goody Goody'
I see some free-boody
And he probed it one-sixth of a meter

There once was a man named Spicolli
Who like to jack with his Ravioli
Loved boy's salad to toss
And drink their sauce
While holding his beefy stombolii

That is no comet you see hurling past Mars
But the jubilant wife of the giant man Lars
She applied proper torque
Until he popped his cork
Then she launched into orbit among the stars

There was a young man from Rabaul
Who had a rectangular ball
The square of his date
plus his penis times eight
Was two-fifths of five-eights of fuck all.

Tarzan swing through the air
Natives see his arse is bare
Tarzan go home to good wife Jane
His noble face fill with pain
How say he lose her underwear?

There was a young girl from Coleshill
Who sat one day on a moleshill
The resident mole
stuck his nose up her hole
Now Miss Coleshill alright but the mole's ill

There was a young lady from Phoenix,
Who stuffed her brassiere with some Kleenex.
She paid it no mind,
Since her boyfriend, in kind,
Used Scott Towels to augment his penix!

There lived a saintly girl from Sleepy Hollow
Who entertained the numerous men of the Wallow
When asked by Ichabod Crane:
"Have you a place I might drain?"
"No Thanks," she replied "I don't Swallow."

There once was a man from Wisconsin
Who had a three foot long johnson
While milking his cow
He fell on his plow
And now sex is no fun

The passengers all were delighted,
The stewardesses too were excited,
Up there in the void,
They really enjoyed
The pleasure of flying United!

A hapless young laddie from Poole
Had a nut on the end of his tool
When he went to unscrew it
His Pa said "dont do it,
or your arse will fall off, you young fool"!

An old mathmetician named Hall
Wrote a theorom not hard to recall

To prove it was wrong
That the length of his Schlong
Was four fifths of five eighths of Fuck All

There once was a man named Brewster,
Who said to his wife as he goosed her,
That used to be grand,
But just look at my hand,
Your not wiping as good as you used to!

The general commanding Fort Totten
Had a habit both snobbish and rotten:
He made men of high ranks
Open left and right flanks
While their privates were mostly forgotten.

There once was a girl who said, "No"
and all the boys called her a "Ho"
and when she was asked why
she simply replied
I have a warm dildo at home.

A young lady from Ashton Le Stairs
Had five large breasts and seven small spares
there were four in a line
the effect was divine
whilst the others were formed up in squares

There was a young man from Atlantis
Who took off an Amazon's panties
And took her to bed
Where she cut off his head
But he carried on, just like a Mantis

There was once a sailor from whales,
An Expert at pissing in gales,
He could piss in a jar
from the top-gallent spar.
Without even wetting the sails.

There was an old lady from Wheeling.
Who had a peculiar feeling.
She laid on her back
And opened her crack
And pissed all over the ceiling

There was an old lady of Ypres
Who got shot in the ass by some snipers,
And when she blew air
Through the holes that were there,
She astonished the cameron pipers.

I sat by the Dutches at tea
and she asked, "Do you fart when you pee?"
I said with some wit,
"Don you belch when you shit?
And felt it was one up for me.

There was an old scholar named Nick
who wrote latin and greek with his prick.
He peed a pecan
in the snow by a john
in a script more than three inches thick

There was a young woman from Wild
Who kept herself quite undefiled
By thinking of Jesus,
Contagious diseases,
And the bother of having a child.

As Titian was mixing rose madder
He spied a young nude on a ladder.
Her position, to Titian,
Suggested coition,
So he climbed up the ladder and had 'er.

There once was a guy named Dane,
Who liked to sing in the rain.

He made fun of an old man,
Who's name was Dan,
But then he got beat with a cane!

There once was a man named Keith
Who circumcised men with his teeth
He didn't do it for leisure
Or sexual pleasure
But did it for the cheese underneath

A sultan who likes his girls buxom
At ninety still often abducts 'em
And then they are led
To a sumptuous bed
In which he regretfully tucks 'em.

There once was a man from South Ealing
Who found his prick highly appealing
But not to feel dumb
He made his hand numb
So it was like someone else he was feeling

I knew an old geezer named Caesar
He tried O his darndest to please her
Though overly stout
And well-known as a lout
He managed to tickle and tease her !

I once knew a dame from Poughkeepsie
Who tucked away bootlegg-ed whiskey
She stuffed all her hockings
Beneath her blue stockings
One nip of her tuck made him tipsy !

There once was a virgin at Penn State
Whose hunger just would not abate.
He said with a grin,
What a sin it'd have been
If I ate out my date on a plate.

There once was a woman named Patti ,
Who was concerned about being a fatty,
She met a man named Garry,
Who was really quite scary,
And he bopped the fatty, off Patti !!

There once was a man from New York
Whose penis was shaped like a fork.
While screwing his wife,
Who was shaped like a knife
They could carve up a really nice pork!

A young lady was fond of a stunt
so she took of her clothes in a punt
she uncorked some Champaign
and without any shame
she sprayed it all over her front

A young lady with dubious style
liked to take off her clothes for a while
she'd get down on her knees
and mainly to please
she'd show off her verticle smile

A girl with magnificent tits
when dancing would wiggle her hips
a wonderful flirt
she'd lift up her skirt
and exhibit her sensuous lips

there was a young man named boc
who had a seventy inch cock
he fell off a chair
poll vaulted through the air
now he can wank with a sock!!

there was a young man who sent e-mails,
to various dubious females,

when axked what they said,
he just shook his head,
i'd rather not go into details.

To the penis of old Mr. Schuster
Was attached an electrical booster
In a screw with Miss Drew
his main rheostadt blew
and it felt like a snowblower had goosed her!

There once was a guy named Dave
Who wanted a good close shave.
His razor did stick,
He cut off his dick
And now he's a eunich slave!

There was a man called Motar
who often rode on a scooter
His favorite trick
was to stand on his prick
and use his arse as a hooter

A Lady asked me to tea
and said "do you fart when you pee?"
I said with some whit
"do you belch when you shit?"
I think that was one up to me

There was a young girl from Utoxeter
so pretty that men waved their cocks at her
one went so far
as to wave from his car
a cock all riddled with pox at her

There once was a troubadour named Gibbon
who did sing for a livin'
I onced asked him why
this was his reply

"I just do it to meet horny women."

There once was a slut named Bobby
Who was blowing a boy named Robie
When I told her to stop
His penis she droped
"But this is my favorite hobby!"

A certain young lady named Allus
Lunched with the king at the Pallus
The dirty old twat
Said look what ive got
And promptly showed her his phallus

There once was a man from Iran,
Who fried his nuts in a pan,
He said with a shout,
"PUT THE FIRE OUT!"
And he went running to his girlfriend Ann.

There was a young girl from Australia,
who painted her cunt like a Dahlia.
At 5 pence a smell,
it was all very well,
but 10 pence a lick was a failure.

There once was a girl called Kim,
who had an allmighty quim.
It wasn't the size
that attracted the flies,
but the crystalized cum round the rim.

There was a young lady named Beti
Who was having sex with a Yeti
When they started to cum
The resulting hum
Upset the scanners at Seti

A dominant lady named Yael
Liked to beat on her slaves with a flail
Sayin' "Be lookin cute,
While you're lickin' my boot,
And continue on up to my tail!"

One evening with forethought and malice
A horny gal travelled to Dallas
She liked to play cowboy
Saying, "hey, you be my boy
Just bring on the whips and your phallus!"

Though she knew it had grown to a fetus.
She felt rumblings come not from her uterous,
So the pregnancy thought,
Was a pregnancy not.
It was really her stomach quite tumorous.

I knew a Jess looking for laboar.
So I said she should be a proffessore.
But the Mrs. Resources
Said "Whoa! Hold your horses"
We don't hire no dopped up old crack whores.

I once knew a Christiane Why,
Who though tried couldn't satisfy guys.
Then a Calvin she met
Who said "Girl, don't you fret.
You won't gag my inadequate size."

There was once a beautiful palace,
'Side the sea, with a vine covered trellis.
And where?.. ..Up beyond,
Yonder oaks, leafy frond,
Rose a turret, tall, shaped of mine phallus.

A girl I once knew named Melania,
Used to lick her own boobs with her tongue, yeah!
But she'd suck them too hard,

For one day, on her yard,
They sprayed milk out, don't get any on ya!

there was a young caveman named Ug
who stuck his plug in a jug.
said ug with a shrug
as he gave it a tug,
'Now ain't this a hell of a fug'

I wooed a stewed nude in Bermuda,
I was lewd, but my God! she was lewder.
She said it was crude
To be wooed in the nude-
I pusued her, subdued her, and screwed her!

There once was a man from Goshem
Who took out his balls to Wash'em
His wife said JACK
If you don't put em BACK
I'll stand on the buggers and squash em

There was an old man on a bench
Who created a terrible stench
He had hairs up his nose
Where grass sometimes grows
And his wife was a stupid old wench

Charlotte the harlot from hell
said, "I wish my body would sell,
But it seems that no buyer,
Is filled with desire,
By the peculiar way that I smell"

"I have serviced this town for years,
Since the days that gays were just queers
I provided most of the gentry,
With their first entry,
And now all I hear are their jeers".

Bill, an Arkansian president,
While in the White House resident,
Did his staff of office display,
In a most unusual way,
Then claimed it was JFK's precedent.

There was a young girl of Surrey
Who only ate spicy curry
She tried a pie and
Stuck it up her nigh
That weird young lady of Surrey

There once was a girl from New York
whose vagina was plugged with a cork.
To remove it she fingered,
but still the cork lingered.
So she got it out with a fork.

There once was a girl from Manila,
who had a face that looked like Godzilla.
She could screw you real fine,
while swinging from a vine,
and give you head just like a gorilla.

There once was a girl from Tucker
Who wanted a canary to pluck her
She tightly squeezed her "Vaginer"
But it flew up her "Hiner"
And was killed by a runnaway trucker

There was a young man from Stroud,
Who was feeling his date in a crowd,
When a man up in front,
went," Sniff, sniff, Cunt!"
Just like that, not loud.

there was a young girl from East Cheam
who crept into the vestry unseen
she took down her knickers

and likewise the vicar's
and said "how about it old bean".

There once was a boy named ali
He took all the girls with glee
But when they unzipped his fly
he wanted to die
cuz his wee was the size of a flea

There once was a girl named Robyn
every night her bed was a bobbin'
the men would take leave
after being quite pleased
and leave Robyn with her body a throbbin'

long ago once in ancient Japan
was a geisha who dressed as a man
her pants were so tight
that they rubbed her just right
when she walked you might say that she ran

A masturbating gourmand from Hanoi
With a tool that resembled Bok Choi
What came in his hand
Looked like Moo Goo Gai Pan
So he garnished it with duck sauce and soy

The bishop one Sunday, in the lurch
After eating a pound of spoiled perch
Emitted a blast
In the middle of mass
That extinguished all the candles in church

A strapping fellow from Australia
After his fortnightly bacchanalia
Buggered a dog
Three mice and a frog
And a bishop in fullest regalia

My tool, it was a throbbin'
and I needed a knobbin'
but being at work
I weren't free to jerk
so I dreamed of Carole's head bobbin'

There once was a young idler named Blood
Made a fortune performing at stud
With a fifteen-inch peter
A double-beat metre
And a load like the Biblical Flood

I think the feeling is grand
Of holding my gland in my hand
But what I really want to do
Is become Johnny Apple-goo
And spread my seed all over the land

There once was a man from Manila
who lived with 5 girls in a villa.
When they'd go to bed
they loved giving head
cause he'd soak it all day in vanilla.

The tale of the chef from France
A victim of drunk circumstance
Though he burned the baguette
What he lived to regret
Was the loaf that he pinched in his pants

The inventor from India said
"I made a turbin from butter instead!"
To the Punjab's surprise
When his pancakes arrived
They served them on top of his head

'Tis a legend in all of Madras
The lass with the breasts of glass
In a sad twist of fate

She fought with her mate
And they smashed when she fell on her ass

Of the indian man Sanjay
Who ate too much curry one day
Though he crapped in Bopahl
It is said by them all
That it stunk all the way to Bombay!

The legend of Indian Chief Eno
Said "thank God they don't know what we know...
Don't fight the white man
Just give 'em the land
Fuck 'em, we'll start a casino!!"

The overweight lady named Tammy
Fell in the ochestra pit in Miami
All of the brass
Went straight up her ass
She farted, and she won a Grammy!!

An alien cam down here from Venus.
Not a girl, but a guy (had a penis).
With three eyes in between,
Pointed ears that were green.
He was obviously not of our Genus.

He landed at old Johnson's farm.
An arrival that caused some alarm
To old Johnson's daughter.
Who thought if he caught her.
He might want to cause her some harm

Now our alien wasn't too bright.
He forgot to bring something to light
The night and his way
Through the field filled with hay
Took a left instead of a right.

Now things didn't turn out like they aughter
He did not meet up with the daughter
Instead he found Bessie
And now things get messy.
He not only found her but caught her.

"My Dear you have beautiful eyes!"
"Big and brown like Venutian Creme Pies"
"I can't wait to show mother
Your soft silky utter."
(You're going to be such a surprise.)

From behind the clouds came the moon,
As the alien continued to spoon.
And old Johnson's girl
Let the curtains unfurl
To a scene that made her heart swoon.

See the alien was wearing no frock
And Ms. Johnson was given a shock
She believed not her eyes
For there 'tween his thighs
Was an 18 inch glowing green cock.

And so to the steps she alighted.
There were things she just knew must be righted
Tell this guy with the cow
Just exactly how
With her he'd be truly delighted.

She ran through the field up to him.
Stuck her hand out and said "My name's Kim"
And you sir are hot
Look here what I got
For you. It's a seldom used quim.

"I'm sorry deary but right now.
I am currently courting this cow."
The alien said

Then Kim nearly dropped dead
(Oh my god he just licked his eye brow)

Now Kim was determined as ever
To succeed in this lustful endeavor
And spend the whole night
In the blissful delight.
She was sure the alien would deliver.

She was sure he'd see Bess was a dud.
Just standing there chewing her cud.
It soon became plain
His lust she'd not gain.
Cause he started in pounding his pud.

But it was the last thing that she saw
That for Kim was the camel's last straw
The alien's tongue
Licked Bess's bung
And a smile split the alien's maw.

Oh Bessie my dear let's make haste
To Venus there's no time to waste
That taste oh..oh my!
Venutian creme pie!
And to the space ship the two raced.

Into the welkin they shot
Leaving poor Kim really hot
For and 18 inch dick
And a tongue oh so quick
So she laid down and played with her twat.

There once was a girl named Spears
Who wanted to enlarge her brassieres
she went to get it
and yup you bet it
now its timblerlake and Spears

There once was a man from Lancaster
who, while eating, befell a disaster
his bowels, well loaded
swelled up and exploded
and filled his nice knickers with plaster

There once was a girl from Kentucky
who considered herself quite lucky.
She'd unzip the fly
of just any old guy
and never found one that was yucky

I'm Darwin, I had an erection
Of several square inches cross-section
So I set out to screw
Every Duchess I knew
In the interest of natural selection

The Queen and the Duke were dismayed,
to find Andy and Koo had once played.
As for Charlie and Ed,
well, enough has been said
'bout the damsels that they might have layed.

In anything written by Dickens,
It's certain the plot always thickens;
With characters, themes
And digressions it teems;
As for sex, though, it's mighty slim pickin's.

At a meeting-hall, George Bernard Shaw
Was proceeding to lay down the law,
When, from somewhere offstage,
Someone hollered in rage,
"Who can sleep, with this damned foo-fa-raw??"

Miss Fanny, adored by John Keats,
Loved romances and sucking on sweets;
Yet one glance from this skirt

Could reduce the poor squirt
To a few inarticulate bleats.

My trouser-snake stands up and cheers
When confronted with boobs in brassieres;
But, in charming my cobra,
The bosom with no bra
Can almost reduce it to tears.

Said the Cardinal to Mother Superior
"Your singing is quite inferior!"
She,not to be crass,
did show some real class
Said,"You can kiss my posterior!"

There once was a boy named Kevin
Who used a vacuum to stretch it to seven,
Then eight and then nine,
And though ten was divine,
There will be film at eleven.

There once was a girl from Norway
Who hung from her toes in the doorway.
She said to her beau,
Hey, look at me Joe,
I think I've found one more way!

in the garden of eden lay Adam
gently stroking his madam,
and great was his mirth
for on all of this earth
there were only two balls and he had 'em!

An Argentine Gaucho named Bruno
Said Sex is one thing I do know
Women are fine
And sheep are divine
But llamas are numero uno!

There once were two young girls from Birmingham
I knew a wild story concerning 'em
They lifted the frock
And diddled the cock
Of the Bishop engaged in confirming 'em

Now the Bishop was nobody's fool,
He'd been to a fine public school
He lowered his britches
And fucked both those bitches
With his twelve-inch Episcopal tool.

But that didn't startle these two,
Why they laughed as the Bishop withdrew,
The Vicar is quicker
And thicker and slicker
And longer and stronger than you!

There once was a man from Bombay
Who fashioned a cunt out of clay
But the heat from his prick
Turned the damn thing to brick
And it ripped all his foreskin away.

There once was a vampire from France
Who couldn't keep it tucked in his pants
He oft whipped it out
With a vampiric shout
And taught poor Louis how to dance.

There once was a man named Piatt,
who's sexual habits were a riot.
From horses to hens,
To mice and men,
If it had a hole, he would try it.

There once was a man named Eugeene,
Who built a masturbation machine,
The damned thing broke

On the 14th stroke,
And whipped his balls to a cream.

Remember that man named Eugeene?
well he built a f*!king machine,
Concave or convex,
It could take any sex,
But man what a mother to clean

There was a lady from Vanvaper
Who wiped her butt with brown paper;
The paper was thin,
Her fingers slipped in,
She no longer used that brown paper.

Jolly St. Nick's good to you and me
Brings to homes many gifts to see.
But a black eye he paid
Because he laid
The wrong doll under the tree.

There Once was a sailor named Brett
The best pisser I ever seen yet
He could Piss in a jar
From the Top Gallant Spar
Nor even get the sails wet.

There once was a man who was not very kind,
he used his penis instead of his mind,
one day he bent over,
and his dog took over,
a gave him a bone from behind.

There once was a man from Peru,
who fell asleep in a canoe,
while dreaming of venus,
he played with his penis,
and woke up with a hand full of goo.

There once was a nun with a gun,
Who thought shooting children was fun,
she shot them away,
Day after day,
Until she thought she was done.

There once was a man from Uppingham
Who stood on the bridge at Buckingham
Just watching the stunts
of the cunts in the punts
And the tricks of the pricks that were fucking them

There once was a monk from Kerplunks
Whose body was that of a hunk's
The nuns all went woozy
when he stepped into the jacuzzi
For the monk had forgotten his trunks.

There was a young lady from Bude
Who had scenes of old England tattooed
Her Boyfriend, one day
went the whole Penine Way
With Cheddar Gorge still to be viewed

There was a young man from Sheet
Who liked to suck on his feet
He'd like to do Fergie
But her feet had the lergie
Because she'd had the entire fleet

There once was a girl from Decator
who was laid by a big alligator
nobody knew
the results of that screw
'cuz after he laid her, he ate her.

There once was a monk from Siberia
Whose manners were quite inferior.
He did to a nun

What he should not have done.
And now she's a Mother Superior.

There was a young lassie named Wainright
Who enjoyed the position that a dog might
over her shoulder she found
when she looked around
A hole new meaning for hindsight

There once was a singer named Elton
who had the girls hearts all a'meltin'.
But soon they discovered
he was a man lover;
twas dicks he'd rather be feltin'.

There was a young singer named M'lisser,
who liked all the girls to kiss her.
She was rakin' the cash in
and givin' tongue lashin's
to Misses rather than Misters.

A young engineer name of Paul
Was equipped with an octagonal ball
The square of his weight
Times his pecker, plus eight
Is his phone number, give him a call

The limerick form is complex
Its contents run chiefly to sex
It burgeons with virgins
And masculine urgins
And swarms with erotic effex.

Sir Reginald Von Hubble of Joice
Did shave his balls-'twas his choice.
He sneezed,oh how sad!
The results were quite bad!
He now has a high pitched voice!!!

There once was a lad called Lancelot
At whom people looked askance a lot
For whenever he passed
A delectable lass
The front of his pant would advance a lot

there once was a guy named scott,
who thought he was SOOO hot,
then Jamie dumped him,
And her new boyfriend thumped him,
Now, a living Scott, there is not.

There was this guy named John
Who's Mom told him to buy some corn.
He heard wrongly
But objected strongly.
When instead he bought some porn.

A psychiatrist and a proctologist from Stutts
Did really show some pure guts.
They put up a sign
At 4th Street and Vine.
That read we treat nuts and butts!

Oh,the air did turn green
When a fart came from the queen!
The court sat aghast
At the royal blast,
But stood and sang "God save the queen!"

There was a young lady from Bath
Who wasn't very good at math
She had sex under a tree
later said "Woe is me"
1 plus 1 isn't 2....it equals 3

Stanley, that anal young fool
made sculptures out of his stool.
His version of "The Thinker"

was really a stinker,
but the portrait of Madonna was cool!

There was a young man from Cape Horn,
who wished he had never been born,
and he wouldn't have been,
if his father had seen
that the tip of the rubber was Torn !

there once was a man named shult
who was a member of a pagan cult
he fell to his knee
and screamed 'help me !'
as the cult sacrificed him 'cause they where hungry

there was a young lady from crewe
who filled her vagina with glue
said she with a grin
if they pay to get in
they'll pay to get out of it, too!

Two moments in Captain Hook's past
memory of which still leave him aghast.
A visit quite vile
from a big crocodile,
and that time he was wiping his ass!

In the check out at the food store
a nun was advising the poor:
"Hey you up in front!
That's to many items you cunt!
And they won't take food stamps for beer ya dumb whore."

A hillbilly gent name of Cato
wanted sex with his girl on a Date-o.
She said, "Yer dick's real purdy,
But yer balls are too dirty,
they look like a fresh dug potato!"

A wandering Munchkin named Syfe
heard a most terrible strife.
The loud grinding and shearing,
lead him to a clearing,
where the Tin Man was fucking his wife.

A genetic engineer named Pickens
gave his lab assistant the dickens!
He had saturated a turd,
with the DNA of some bird,
and got some shit that tastes kinda' like chicken!

A childless man took to chasin'
a curvy young girl with elation.
She asked him "why me?",
he replied, full of glee,
"you were built for the birth of a nation!"

She wanted to grow up a saint
And her mother, she had no complaint
But men--quite a few--
Were more fun than a pew
So she wanted to be but she ain't!

There was a young girl from Calais
Who thought chancres just melted away.
Now she has Tabes,
and sabre-shinned babies,
and thinks that she's Queen of the May.

There once was a lady from Sydney
Who could take it right up to the kidney
Then a man from Quebec
Took it up to her neck
...He had a big one now didn't he

There once was a girl from Aberystwyth
Who took corn to the mill to make grist with.
The miller's son, Jack

Laid her flat on her back
And united the organs they made piss with!

There once was a man from Devizes
Whose balls were of different sizes.
The left one was small,
Hardly nothing at all,
But the other won numerous prizes.

There once was an abbot of Brittany
Who chanted this desolate litany:
"If Christ is the Source
Of Divine Intercourse,
Then how come I don't ever gitany?"

A washed up old harlot named Tupps,
Was heard to confess, in her cups:
"The height of my folly
Was screwing a collie,
But I got a good price for the pups!"

There once was a man named Nute
Who poured acid on his root
He got holes, you see
So when he would pee
He'd finger the thing like a flute!

There once was a man from Kent
Who's dick was so long it was bent
To stay out of trouble,
He stuck it in double
So instead of coming, he went

There was was a man named Molder
Who attempted to throw a small boulder
Instead he tripped on a rock,
And grasped his own cock,
And threw himself over his shoulder.

There once was a man from Iraq
Who had holes down the length of his cock
When he got an erection,
He could play a selection
From Johann Sebastion Bach

The things that occur on the shingle
of the beaches surrounding old Dingle
can only be said
in the bed of the wed
'cause they'd tingle the single to mingle!

There once was a man from Eau Claire
Who diddled his wife in a chair
On the thirtyfirst stroke
the furniture broke
and his gun went off in the air.

There once was a butcher from Clack
Who found slicing meat was his knack
Up until the day
He met his "friend" Ray
Now he only takes meat in the back.

There was also a butcher from here
Who's meat slicing method was queer
He would handle the steak
And cream he would make
As he only took meat in the rear.

A wire-winder who caught his wire in his winder,
Wasn't hurt much and said, "Fate couldn't have been much kinder."
Said his wife, Jane,
"You can say that again",
"Just imagine if you caught it in our meat grinder."

There once was a man from Racine,
Who invented a fucking machine,

concave and convex,
it fucked either sex
and jerked off itself in between.

A father of 3 boys named J. Dickinson
Found incest to be quite a lot of fun.
Said a friend, "Even though J.",
"May be gay",
"At least his name matches his avocation."

A father of 4 girls named Dickinson
Found incest to be quite a lot of fun.
Said a friend, "Maybe we oughter"
"Nickname him Dickindaughter",
"Then that name will match his avocation."

This is the tale of woe of a small boy named Lou
Sitting in a crowded church with his family, who
Turned to his father, Bart,
And whispered, "Dad, I've got to fart !"
Said Bart, "If you do, you must sit in your own pew."

A young woman from the Land Where the Sun Rises
Had boobs of unequal sizes.
The left one was small
And didn't seem abnormal at all,
But the right one was so huge it won prizes.

There once was a Man named McSweeny
Who spilled some Gin on his weenie
Just to be Couth
He added Vermouth
And slipped his chick a Martini!

He invented a sexual device
and tried the thing out once or twice
but it wasn't the gong
but rather his prong
that peeled and that didn't feel nice.

There was a young fellow of Crew
whose tool was so straight and to true
that the Navy when fighting
could use it for sighting
and at full range could sink a canoe.

An observant young man of the west
said "I've found out by personal test
that men who make passes
at girls who wear glasses
get just as good sex as the rest".

A harlot did not think it funny
to hear the bad jokes told by Sonny.
"I will not", she said
"have such filth in my bed"
then she cursed and gave him back his money.

A toothsome young starlet named Smart
was asked to display oral art
as the price for a role.
She complied, met his goal
and then sank her teeth in the part.

There was a young harlot of Clyde
whose doctor cut open her hide.
He misplaced her stitches
and closed all her niches
she now does her work on the side.

Since her baby came, Miss Snow
won't diddle, she just hollers "no".
She thinks a fat senator
was it's likely progenitor
but having laid ten she can't know.

There was a young lady from Sydney
who could take it right up to her kidney,

but a man from Quebec
put it up to her neck
My, he had a long one, now didn't he.

As the elevator car left our floor
Big Sue caught her chest in the door.
She yelled a good deal,
but had they been real
she'd have yelled considerably more.

A virgin emerged form her bath
in a state of righteous wrath
for she'd been deflowered
when she bent as she showered
'cause the handle was right in her path.

Said a horrid old hag, "Look here honey
I know that I'm wrinkled and funny,
but get me in bed
with a sack on my head
and I'll give you a run for your money".

There was a young lady from Channelview
whose boyfriend said "may I explore you?"
She replied to the chap
"I will draw you a map
where the others have been to before you".

There was an old maid of Duloth
who wept when she thought of her youth
and the glorious chanced
she'd missed at school dances
and once in a telephone booth.

There was a young girl from Balmoral
whose habits were highly immoral.
For the price of a dime
she took three at a time,
one fore, one aft, and one oral.

Said a coed from Duke University
when asked about sexual diversity,
"Screwing's okay
in the old fashioned way,
but I do like a touch of perversity.

There was a young student named Jones
who reduced all maidens to groans
by his wonderful knowledge
acquired in college
of nineteen erogenous zones.

A businesslike harlot named Draper
once tried an unusual caper.
What made it so nice
was you got it half-price
if you brought in her ad from the paper.

A newlywed bride, Mrs. Young
asked the doctor to fix her torn lung.
When asked how it ripped
she replied as she stripped,
"That man I married is hung".

Said a diffident lady named Drood
the first time she saw a man nude,
"I'm glad I'm the sex
that's concave not convex
for I don't fancy things that protrude".

When Smith caught his tool in some gears
they grafted on skin from his ears
and now the poor guy
can hear through his fly,
but screwing just bores him to tears.

There once was a versatile whore
as expert behind as before

For a buck you could view her
for to you could do her
as she stood on her head on the floor.

There once was a faddist of Devon
who said "I have raped only seven
young women to date,
but soon it'll be eight
and shortly thereafter eleven".

A young airline stewardess, May,
has achieved the ultimate lay.
She was screwed without quittin'
from New York to Great Britain
it is clear that she's come a long way.

A horny young sailor named Clark
picked up a slut in a park.
She was ugly and crude
and a horror when nude,
but she was good for a spell in the dark.

There once was a fellow named Mark
who spread a girls legs in the dark
He said "Now by thunder
it's a natural wonder
I declare this a National Park".

There was a young fellow named Dice
who remarked "They say bigamy's nice.
Even two is a bore
I prefer three or four
for the plural of spouse it is spice".

The 80-year-old accused of rape was called Mort,
And the judge said, "Sir, you'll have to be tried in court."
But the jury was sympathetic,
Because Mort was sick, old, and pathetic,
And the evidence wouldn't stand up in court.

There once was a man from Nantucket,
Whose dong was so long he could suck it.
He walked down the street,
Just a swinging his meat.
While he carried he's balls in a bucket.

There was a young man who's dong
Was prodigiously, massively long
Down the sides of his whang,
two testes did hang
Which attracted a curious throng

There was a young lady from China
Who mistook for her mouth, her vagina
Her clitoris huge
she covered with rouge
And lipsticked her labia minor

A geneticist I'll call Dr. Harold Louth
Crossed a rooster with peanut butter from down south.
His friends did query
"And what did you get, Harry ?"
Said he, "A cock that'll stick to the roof of your mouth".

A new graduate gynecologist named Scott
Found he knew diddly squat
About sex, because he'd never
Been so clever
As to go out on a date that was hot.

There was a hooker from Honchu
Who on peckers and penises did chew.
Said a friend, "Why don't you
Have them stick it to you,
Then you could enjoy the sex too".

There was a man from Havana,
Who thought he could play the piana

His fingers slipped,
his zipper unzipped.
And out came a hairy banana!

There once was a man from Australia
Who had rather large genitalia
he said to his bride,
don't try to hide
'cause wherever you go I can nail ya'

Said Rapunzel, high up in her castle
"This is getting to be quite a hassle -
I've given up hope
Of a prince with a rope
So I'm growing my hair past my astle"

There once was a kingsnake named Elvis
with a less-than-vestigial pelvis
and the bulge in his jeans
came from twin hemipenes
I'm much too embarrassed to tell this.

There was a young girl from Australia
Who painted her arse like a dahlia
The picture was fine
And the colour device
But the scent on the whole was a failure

There was a young man from Australia
Who painted his ass like a dahlia.
A penny a smell
Was all very well
But twopence a lick was a failure.

A gentle old lady I knew
Was dozing one day in her pew;
When the preacher yelled "Sin!"
She said,"Count me in!
As soon as the service is through!"

There was an old maiden named Grissing
Who discovered what she had been missing.
When she laid down on the sod,
She cried out,"Oh,Dear God!
All these years I just used it for pissing!"

There was an old man named Ringer,
Was seducing a beautiful singer.
He said with a grin,
"Now,I've got it in."
She said,"You mean that's not your finger?"

There was a young lady from Cheshire
Who succumbed to her lover's desire
She said,"It's a sin,
But now that it's in,
Could you shove it a few inches higher?"

There once was a fellow named Skinner,
Who took a lady to dinner to winner,
At half-passed nine,
They started to dine,
At half-passed ten, it was inner.

The hygienic young miss from out west
Ask the cowboy who sat on her chest
"Will cum cause decay?"
No m'am I've heard say
It's the secret ingredient of Crest

There once was a man named frisk
Whose stroke was exceedingly brisk
So fast was his action
That the lorenze contraction
Turned his tool into a disk

there once was a man from china
who wasn't a very good climber

he slipped on a rock
and broke his cock
and now he's got a vagina

There was a young woman of Croft
who played with herself in the loft
having reasoned that candles
could never cause scandals
besides which they never go soft.

There was a young sailor named Fred.
He once took a mermaid to bed.
He said, to be blunt,
"I can't find your cunt,
so why don't you blow me, instead!"

A fellow from out near Pike's peak,
Stood up in a large crowd to speak,
Got a tear in his eye,
When he noticed his fly,
Had been opened since he last took a leak.

There once was a naval cadet
who's dreams where usually wet
when dream't of his wedding
he soaked up the bedding
and the wedding aint taken place yet!!!

There was a young lady of Wheeling
Who claimed to lack sexual feeling.
Then, a cynic named Boris
Just *touched* her clitoris.
She had to be scraped from the ceiling.

Please pity the Duchess of Kent!
Her pussy's so dreadfully bent
That the poor wench doth stammer
"I need a sledgehammer
To pound a man into my vent".

There was a young lady of Exeter,
So pretty that men craned their necks at her.
One was even so brave
As to take out and wave
The distinguishing mark of his sex at her.

There was an old hermit named Dave
Who kept a dead whore in a cave.
He said "I admit
I'm a bit of a shit
But think of the money I save".

Well the Mayor of the town took the floor
Said "his actions we simply deplore -
That old hermit named Dave
With the whore in the cave,
We can't tolerate this anymore."

The poor girl named Nell, has to go
But it raises a problem, I know
When Dave needs to screw
Just what will he do,
When he's horny and ain't got no dough?

So the townfolk all chipped in a buck
Even those who were down on their luck.
To get poor old Dave
From that stinking old cave
Into town for a really good f***

They went to see Dave the next day
And said they were willing to pay
One hundred a week
If only he'd seek
A live whore he wanted to lay.

Dave liked their offer real well
And said he would bury dead Nell

In a hole in the ground
And put flowers all around.
Besides, she had started to smell.

Then he found him a Nympho, named Grace.
For a hundred she'd move to his place.
One day they found Dave
Stone cold dead in his cave
With a beautiful smile on his face.

There was a girl from Lop Nor
who unfortunately couldn't score.
To please her socket,
she mounted a rocket
and came with a colossal roar

There once was a science teacher
Who's father's job was a preacher
She'd give out her thesis
While preaching of Jesus
And how God created all creatures

That teacher, she had broken a rule
You can't teach religion in school
She lost her job
And without a sob
She challenged her boss to a duel

She took the case to a judge
But the court just wouldn't budge
She was good in her schooling
She hated the ruling
So she gave her boss the nudge

She was tried and convicted for murder
And was placed behind the steel girders
Of a state prison
For teachin' religion
And that murder most certainly hurt her

And that's the rest of my story
For the rest is really quite boring
You'd find it real crude
And terribly rude
And you might fall asleep, and start snoring!

There once was a man from Franzini,
Who spilled some Gin on his weenie,
Not being uncouth,
He added Vermouth,
And slipped his date a Martini!

There once was a fair young lass
Her body was made out of glass
From there you could note
What went on in her throat
and all the way down to her ass.

All men seem to be one of a kind
They'll make love just for fun, but you'll find
Women are not just about
To consider it without
Some ulterior motive in mind.

There was a young barmaid at sail
Tattooed on her chest the price of Ale
And on her behind
For the the blind
the same, but in brail

There once was a lady from France,
who decided she'd just take a chance.
So she let herself go
for an hour or so,
and now all her sisters are aunts!!

there was a young girl from Hong Kong
who said "you are utterly wrong"

to say my vagina's
the biggest in china
just because of your mean little dong

There was a teenager named Donna
who never said no, I dont wanna
two days out of three
she'd shoot LSD
and on weekends, she smoked marijuana

there was a young man named dave
who kept a dead whore in a cave
he said what the hell,
you get used to the smell
and think of the money I save

there was a young girl from Seville
who used dynamite for her thrill
they found here vagina
in North Carolina
and parts of her tits in Brazil

there once was a girl from Nantucket
who crossed the sea in a bucket
and when she got there
they asked for the fare
so she pulled up her dress and said fuck it

There was a man from Madras,
Who fucked a young girl in the grass.
But the hot Spanish sun
Spoiled half his fun
By burning the skin on his ass !

There once was a man from Bel Air.
He wanted to fuck a bear.
He pulled down his pants,
He began to romance,
Now he has one ball and some hair.

There once was a lad from the sea.
He fucked a baboon in a tree.
The result was quite horrid,
All ass and no forehead,
Four balls and a purple goatee.

Did you hear about young Henry Lockett?
He was blown down the street by a rocket.
The force of the blast
Blew his balls up his ass,
And his pecker was found in his pocket.

There once was a harlot named Leeza
Who said, "If my cunt doesn't please ya,
You can cum
In my slimy old bum,
Just be careful the tapeworm don't seize ya".

There once was a woman from France
Who got on the bus in a trance.
Six passengers fucked her,
Besides the conductor,
And the driver shot twice in his pants.

There once was a princess of Saboda.
She built an erotic pagoda.
The walls of its halls
Are festooned with the balls
And the tools of the fools that bestrode her.

To his bride, said the lynx-eyed detective,
"Could it be that my eyesight is defective?
Has your east tit the least bit
Bested the west tit,
Or is it a trick of perspective?".

There once was a fellow named Sweeney.
His girl was a terrible meanie.

The hatch to her snatch
Had a catch that would latch--
She could only be screwed by Houdini.

The office of oral surgeon Dr. Rob Guild
Was next to that of gynecologist Dr. Bob Gild.
One day, a new patient of Rob's, Ms. Blake
Entered the wrong office by mistake
Was asked to undress, did so, and said, "I need 2 pulled and
1 filled".

There was a boy named Roy,
who married the queen of Troy.
Oh! What a dame;
she put him to shame,
by fiddling with his little toy!

There once was a Queen of Bulgaria
whose bush had grown hairy and hairier
'Til a Prince from Peru
Came up for a screw
had to hunt for her cunt with a terrier!

There once was a pervert named Bob
who wanted a blow job.
He found a snapping turtle
whose name was Mirtil
and now he carries a corncob.

Governor Willy's face got quite red
When he said, "Paula, give me some head."
He pulled down his pants,
And expected romance,
But Miss Jones sued his dumb ass instead.

There once was a man from Dundee,
Who molested an ape in a tree,
The result was most horrid,

All arse and no forehead,
Three balls and a purple goatee!

There was a young woman named Cindy,
Whose breasts were as small as can be,
So to the doctor she went,
With an attitude hell-bent,
To go from an "A" to a "D".

The surgery's done, now it's time for some fun,
Even though they are still kind of smartin',
Now the saline's in place,
And with a smile on her face,
They resemble that of Dolly Parton.

We try to be kind, but you must keep in mind,
As we say now in verses and rhymes....
Every time you bend over,
To pick up that clover,
That gravity sure sucks sometimes.

With summer a commin', I wouldn't try running
On days that are sunny and hot,
But when your boyfriend comes pouncing,
And boy are they bouncing,
They still will be comfortable...NOT!!!

Now this may be a quirk, but if this doesn't work,
You can still take your doctor to court....
You can say that he lied,
And your living bra had just died,
and you're suing for lack of support!!

Said oul Kate to her crock of a Kettle,
Sure you're not in the finest of fettle,
But your spout isn't slack,
like my poor husband Jack,
Pity his wasn't made out of metal!

There once was a woman named Gladys,
Who had excessive flatus.
She ditched legumes,
Reduced her fumes,
And preserved her olfactory apparatus.

There once was a man from Nantucket
Who stuck his Dork in a socket
His wife was a bitch
She turned on the switch
And his Dork flew off like a rocket!

There once was a girl from Rino
Who used to love playing Keno
She laid on her back
and opened her crack
Now she owns the Casino

There once was a lady from New Zealand
Who was put in jail for stealin'
She laid on her back
She opened her crack
And pissed all over the ceiling

Said a thoughtful young stud from Brazilia
"One orgasm spasm will fill ya
I'll just let the rest
Gush out on your chest
If I shot it inside,it'd kill ya!

There once was a man from Bombay.
He molded a c*nt out of clay.
The heat from his d*ck
Made it turn to a brick,
And it chafed all his foreskin away.

There was a young man from Newcastle,
Who wrapped up some shit in a parcel,
He sent it to Spain,

With a note to explain,
That it came from his grand mothers arse hole

There was a young man from Bullosham,
Who took out his balls just to wash 'em,
His wife said Jack,
if you don't put them back,
I'll tread on the bastards and squash 'em!

There once was a boy named Chris
And everyone thought he was a priss
In sheer desperation
he underwent a sex change operation
and he went from a mister to a miss

There was a young vampire called mable
whose periods were particularly stable
by the light of the moon
with the aid of a spoon
she could drink herself under the table

If you can't dip your wick in a WAC
Or ride the Breast of a WAVE
Squat in the sand
Do it by hand
Think of the money you save!

There once was a queen, who with malice,
Took a leak in the king's favorite chalice,
That woman he'd bedded
Has since been beheaded,
And now he's alone in the palace.

There once was a young man named Brewster
who said to his wife as he goosed her,
"This used to be grand,
but look at my hand,
you're not wiping as clean as you used ta'"

There once was a lady from Niger
Who had an affair with a tiger
The result of the fuck
Was a bald headed duck
Two gnats and a circumcised spider

There once was a young man named Chuck
Who found a young girl out of luck
She started to dance
So he pulled down his pants
Then she hit him when he didn't duck!

When teaching some econ one day
A professor was heard to then say
When supply meets demand
Then all through the land
No one has to be alone when they play!

There once was a woman named Sue
Who gave blow jobs 'till she was blue
When an earthquake hit
She bit into it
Now her lover is a girl too!

there once was an old lady named mable
in bed she had proved herself able
she fucked like a bunny
called her men sonny
while bent over the dining room table.

There was a young lawyer quite bright
Couldn't fuck cause her twat was too tight
She discovered a loophole
By using her poophole
Now she fucks all day and night

There once was a man from Leene,
Who invented a pleasure machine.
Concave or convex,

It fit either sex,
And attachments for those in between

There was once a man from Bombay
who fashioned a cunt out of clay
but the heat of his prick
made it into a brick
and chafed his foreskin away

There once was a man from St. Paul
Who liked to do tricks in the hall
His favorite trick
was to stand on his prick
And roll around on his balls

There once was a man named Dina
Who was in search of the perfect vagina
Everyday he would hunt
For this flawless cunt
I'm flattered, because it was mine-a!!!

There once was A young maid from Aberwristwith
who took corn to the mill to make grist with
the millers son jack
laid her flat on her back
and they joined up the parts that they pissed with

There was a young girl named Mellisse
from Canada who liked to kiss
but it's girls she adores
not men in their drawers
cause they smell and they stand up to piss

I once knew a man from leur,
He seemed to be very poor,
He won a great sum,
But fell on his bum,
And landed in a pile of manure.

I met a lady from Maine,
Who seemed to be insane
She tripped on her shoe,
And fell into some poo
Now she's insane with a stain.

I remember a fellow named Louie,
Who ate 17 bowls of chop- suey,
When the eighteenth was brought,
He became overwrought,
And we watched as poor Louie went Blooie!!

A man with throbbing erection
who had forgotten sexual protection,
took a roll on the floor
with a questionable whore,
and now has a nasty infection.

There once was a president named Billy,
Whose sexual prowess to me seemed quite silly,
Till he was sued,
It was us who was screwed,
By all the young girls sucking his Willie!

One morning Mahatama Gandhi
Had a hard on and it was a dandy
He said to his aide
"Please bring me a maid,
Or a goat, or whatever is handy!"

There once was a young man from Eiling
who pounded his pud with great feeling
And then like a trout
he'd stick his mouth out
and wait for the drops from the ceiling

There once was a man from Rangoon,
who was born 9 months too soon.
He didn't have the luck

to be born by a fuck.
He was scraped off the sheets with a spoon.

There was a fellow from Chanute
Who was troubled by warts on his root.
He put acid on these
and now when he pee's
He toodles his root like a flute.

T'was a fair lass named Sher,
Would do most anything on a dare,
For when the wind blew,
As her lover's well knew,
Her skirts were well worth the stare!

As she was grasping his bum
Bill said 'Please swallow my come'
but all the mess
dripped down her dress
Now Ken Star sez he's a bum

There once was a perv named Steve,
Who liked to play with branches and leaves.
He shoved up his rectal,
A twig-like projectile,
But instead of getting hard he was peeved.

There once was a man from Birritz
Who planted an acre of tits
They came up in the fall
Red nipples and all
And he promptly chewed them to bits

Once the president went to Nantucket
And he wanted a girl to f'ck it
The girl said NO
'cause she's no hoe
He said "OK Just Suck it!!"

There once was a maid in Vancouver
Whose mouth was a twenty horse Hoover
She did her jobs well
But men found they were hell
Once she finished they couldn't remove her

A man named Morgan, its known,
Was threatened should he grow a bone
While away from his wife
She'd brandish a knife
Cut it off and freeze for her own.

There once was a fellow named Leland,
whose balls hung from here to New Zealand.
Both the North and the South
would fit in his mouth.
Which kept him perpetually kneelin'

There once was a man made of tin,
with no heart beneath his grey skin.
By a shear stroke of luck,
he learned how to fuck,
and lived merrily in a world full of sin.

There once was a fellow named Becker.
Who had purple scabs on his pecker.
When scraped by his truss,
they oozed yellow puss.
For certain, and intercourse wrecker.

There once was a fellow named Fong
Who's pecker was seven feet long.
It was bronzed when he died,
For the Church of Saint Clyde,
Where it's now a bell clapper, ding dong!

There once was a gay fellow named Dan
he was fixing his lowriding van,
When the belt of his garter

got caught on the starter,
he screamed and the shit hit the fan!

There was a fat lady from china
Who had an enormous vagina
And when she was dead
They painted it red
And used it for docking a liner.

There once was a priest from St. Giles,
Who's arse was too wide for the aisles.
To and from mass,
The pews pinches his ass.
And gave him a case of the piles.

There once was a priest from Gibraltar.
Who buggered a nun on the altar.
"Now look what you've done!"
Exclaimed the nun.
"You've gummed up the leaves of the psalter!"

There once was a man from Peru
who lived in a one man canoe
while dreaming of venus
and stroking his penis
he woke up with a handful of goo

There once was a fellow named Bruno
Who said "About fucking, I do know
A camel is fine,
An alpaca divine,
But a llama is numero uno."

There once was a man named Jim
Who mounted a girl named Kim
When he entered her cunt
He gave a great grunt
She said, "Oh how you've grown Tim."

There once was a girl named Louise
Who's cunt hair hung past her knees
The fleas on her box
Tied her hair up in knots
And now it's a flying trapeze

There once was a man from Cape Fear;
who had a dick for an ear.
He said " Sex could last long
 if you're neck's good and strong,
just don't get your ear caught in your zipper".

There was a young maid from Norway
Who hung by her heels in a doorway
She said to her beau
Look here, Joe
I think I've found one more way.

There once was a queer named Taylor
who seduced a very young sailor
They threw him in jail
but he worked out his bail
by doing his thing on the jailer

There was an old lady from Kent
To the football game she went
As she sat on the goal
and opened her hole
Guess where the football went

There once was a lady named Dot
who inserted a fly up her twat
that fucker would buzz,
way down in her fuzz
till you glued his wings tight with a shot

there once was a man from Iraq
who had holes down the length of his cock
when he got an erection,

he would play a selection
from Johan Sabastian Bach

At first when i met you at the bar
I couldn't help but tell you how fucking fat you are
But i like the way you make your titi's shake
And if you lost a little weight
You could look like Ricki Lake

Ethnologists up with the Sioux
Wired home for two punts, one canoe.
The answer next day
Said, "Girls on the way,
But what in the hell's a panoe?"

There was a young girl of Darjeeling
Who could dance with such exquisite feeling
There was never a sound
For miles around
Except fly-buttons hitting the ceiling.

There was a young girl of Samoa
Who plugged up herself with a boa.
This strange contraceptive
Was very deceptive
To all but the spermatozoa.

There once was a plumber named Lee
Who was "plumbing" his wife by the sea.
She said, "Stop your plumbing,
I hear someone coming!"
He said, "Yes I know dear, it's me!"

There was a young lady named Alice
Who peed in the Archbishop's chalice.
When asked to explain
She said with disdain,
" 'Twas from need, not from Protestant malice."

Said Slick Willy to the young Paula Jones,
I'd like to listen to your sighs and your moans.
So if you have the nerve
To deep throat this curve
It will tickle your erogenous zones.

Paula Jones proved to be very smart
When asked to perform oral art.
I will not, she said
Put that thing in my head.
Do you think I'm a trailer park tart?

Our gallant young president ,'Slick Willie'
Showed his 'sword' to a sweet young filly.
He said, 'My sword would cut better
If you would give it a header.'
Replied the filly to Willie, 'Don't be silly!'

Slick Willy, with his distinguishing curve
Certainly had an abundance of nerve.
When he ordered: 'Paula, get oral'
She replied, 'Oh no, that's immoral'
And declined his presidential d'oeuvre.

There once was a girl from Brunt
Standing in water up to her knees;
This poem doesn't rhyme yet,
but wait 'tin the tide comes in!

The little green booger-men from Mars
shit in neighborhood bars
"There in the crapper"
they put on the wrapper
Thats how we get cheap cigars

A man of conceit, name of Ryne,
lures girls on to infamous crime.
"I deliver," he boasts,

"two goals and the post,
And goodness knows how many times."

There once was a hillbilly Bill
Who lived on the capitol hill.
He zapped an intern,
Got a media burn
And now his life's going downhill.

there was a man from leeds
who swallowed a packet of seeds
Around his cock
grew Virginia Stock
and out of his ass grew weeds

There was a woman called Jean
In whose knickers many had been
But when she undressed
They thought it was best
To not say what they had seen

There was a young lady from Exeter,
and all the young men threw their sex at her.
Thinking it rude,
she lay in the nude,
while her parrot (a pervert) took pecks at her.

There was a young postman from Hamm
whose ass looked like a delicious ham
when he walked for a mile
you´d see his walking style
that´s why he is called madame.

There once was an under- sexed boy
he hadn´t much fun to enjoy
he died in the night
while a very wild ride
on his monstrous sexual toy

There once was a man named Cleatith
He spent half his life in a pheatith
He had no dick
he looked really sick
and therefore he is not compleatith

There once was a nice guy named Steve
He was a fashionable Taiwanese
He liked handsome boys
And long hard toys
And was quick and ready with a yes please

There once was an undertakers daughter named Maddie
Who befriended a young virgin laddie
She said, "If you do what I say
We'll have a great lay
Since I've buried more stiffs than my daddy"

There once was a man named McNameter
Who was blessed with both length and diameter
But it wasn't his size
that gave them surprise
It was his rhythm iambic pentameter

there was a young woman named Pat,
who offered to do this or that,
when speaking of this,
she meant more than a kiss,
so imagine her meaning of that

There was a young woman from Sweden,
Who didn't much like breast-feedin'.
Unfortunately for her lad
She gave the job to his dad,
But he just ended up bleedin'!

Had an Uncle who lived in Toledo
He tried to live incognito
But he was hung like a horse

Tough to hide it of course
It really screwed up his Libido

There once was a young man named Yost
Who had quite an affair with a ghost
At the height of orgasm
The poor ectoplasm
Cried, "Oh goodie, I feel it...almost."

A swinging young couple from Histwyth
Knew another that they would play whist with
And whenever able
They'd reach under the table
To play with what the other one pissed with

there once was a man from Royce,
He couldn't control his sphincter by choice,
so he rode and he strode
to his favorite commode,
blew his nose blew his ass and rejoiced.

A time long ago in China
There was a man who couldn't be fine-a
He loved sex since he was ten
But it was always with men
Yet he really wanted vagina

There was a young woman from Thrace
Whose corset was too tight to lace
Her mother said, "Nelly
there's more in your belly
I fear than went in through your face".

There once was a man from Caldockery
Who was having a piece on the rockery
She said to her chum,
"You've cum on me bum!
This isn't a Fuck it's a mockery!"

There was a young man of Australia
Who painted his ass like a dahlia:
The drawing was fine,
The painting divine,
But the aroma -- ah, that was the failure.

A comely young widow named Ransom
Was ravished three times in a hansom:
When she cried out for more,
Came a voice from the floor,
"Lady my name is Simpson, not Sampson"

King Henry the Eighth was a Tudor
Of our monarchs we've witnessed fu ludor:
Each wife that he wed,
He led to the bed,
Where he vudor, and wudor, and scrudor.

I wonder how King Arthur felt,
When one day Queen Guinevere knelt,
Saying: "Tell me, my pet,
How did Lancelot get
The key to my chastity belt?"

There was a young maid of Peru
Who swore she never would screw,
Except under stress
Of forceful duress,
Like: 'I'm ready. How about you?'

There was a young nun from Peru
Whom the Bishop wanted to screw,
But she said "The Vicar
Is quicker and slicker,
And three inches longer than you."

There was a young woman from Wheeling
Who I found too be, quite appealing
So I took her home, only to find

This poor girl was out of her mind
She loved too have sex, on the ceiling

Our sax-playing President did plead,
"Paula, please come wet my reed."
I can not comply
She said with a sigh,

There was a young shepherd from Trieste,
Who all his ewe-lambs did molest,
Whilst humping away
One hot summer's day
An old ram ate his shorts and string vest.

There was a young scotsman named Andy,
Who went to a pub for a shandy.
On lifting his kilt
To see what he spilt,
The barmaid said "Blimey - that's handy!"

A red-headed stripper called Sally
Regularly performed at the pallais.
She got such applause
When she dropped her drawers
'Cos the hair on her head did not tally.

There once was a man from Nantucket
Who dropped his dick in a bucket
Along came a guy Dan
Who was a very gay man
So he decided to suck it

Sailor Uranus is a bit of a queer
her friend Sailor Neptune has no fear
because they are lovers
playing under the covers
and all you here is a groan or a cheer

There was a fifteen-year-old named Andy
but no one thought of him as being randy
Girls looking like Venus
gave him a lift of the penis
and one slut-girl said, "Tonight, that'll handy!"

Jack helped Jill mount a horse at a trough
They had so much fun without even a scoff
She said, "I want more
than a ride on a door,
Jack, do I need to help you off?

There was a young lady from Utoxeter,
the boys all waved their cocks at her,
she contracted the pox
from one of the cocks,
Now she's poxed all the cocks in Utoxeter.

There once was an ugly young man
who had good uses for his hand
his fingers were long
and so was his dong
so he always comes again

There once was a man called Bill
Who had his wife, named Hil
Bill, you see,
could not take a pee
For he had no willy

The Right Reverend Dean of St. Just
Was consumed with erotical lust
He buggered three men
Two mice and a hen
And a little green lizard that bust.

There was a woman named Jenny
Whose usual charge was a penny
For half the sum

You could rub off her bum
A source of amusement to many

A girl to her boyfriend did mock,
"Just look at the shape of your cock,
Is it because you are queer
Or those ten pints of beer
That the big hand is at six O'clock."

A horny young lady, Miss Barrett
was caught by her mom in the garret,
she was pushing a diamond
clear up to her hymen
& ramming it home with a carrot.

There once was a comic named Pee Wee
Whose member had the shape of a kiwi
He learned that day
when the cops took him away
That his kiwi could do more than wee-wee

there once was a man named mc Nab
it seems he had the crabs
he shaved under his dick
he grabbed an ice pick
and then he went stab stab stab.

Theres once was a guy named Joe.
His best friend's name was Poe.
The lived together,
In warm and cold weather,
And now they have a son named Moe.

There was once a man named McNair
who tried to intercourse with a bear
that nasty ole brute
took a swipe at his root
and left McNair with one ball and a hair.

There once was a whore in the school
Who thought that it would be cool
To go out and get it
Screwing teachers for credit
What a fucked up fool

There once was a genie with a ten foot wiener
And he showed it to the lady next door
She thought it was a snake
And hit it with a rake
And now its only five-foot-four

There was an old woman of old
Who met a young man quite bold
When she asked, "Why you choose me?"
He replied, "Because lady,
There's simply more of you to hold.

A sexy young girl from Cape Cod
Had to carry her breasts in a hod
Her shape was perfection
and caused many erection
But when she bent over, MY GOD!

A Mormon who moved west to Reno,
Lost his fortune at poker and Keno.
He ran out of luck
And lost his last buck
While drinking some doctored up Vino.

So he married a 21 dealer,
Who was also a very fine peeler.
They moved to Niagra,
And peddled bogus Viagra
To Veterans and surviving New Dealers.

They found profitable professions,
Giving old farts penile erections.
And the company Pfizer,

Was never the wiser,
Despite all the phony prescriptions.

There once was a fellow named latex
who invented a way to have safe sex.
Put a bag on your dick,
any girl you can stick.
But first you must remove the playtex.

While Titian was mixing Rose Madder,
His model was perched on a ladder.
Her sultry position
Inspired coition,
So he nipped up the ladder and had 'er!

There once was a man with a penis disease
When confronted by women he'd get on his knees
He was quite the lover
But allergic to rubber
So he'd beg "can we sixty-nine, PLEASE?!!"

A religious man drowned in a puddle of semen
His dick was possessed by a horrible demon
He'd shoot acid cum
On all the crumb bums
When people saw this they'd run screamin'

In a tub full of jello we'll grope.
For what jiggles or wiggles we'll cope.
Then we'll discover
when you have a lover,
your bodies cum cleaner less soap.

I'm here to show I'm no dupe!
I know what to do with this goop:
When you've a vixen,
just add some friction,
and you can turn jello to soup.

To jello add melons to squeeze,
and cherry red lips wide to please.
In the end comes a stream
of pressurized cream:
Fruit salad to eat from the knees.

There once was a gal named Lewinsky
Who played on a flute like Stravinsky
'Twas "Hail to the Chief"
on this flute made of beef
that stole the front page from Kaczynski.

Said Bill Clinton to young Ms. Lewinsky
We don't want to leave clues like Kaczynski,
Since you look such a mess,
use the hem of your dress
And wipe that stuff off of your chinsky.

Lewinsky and Clinton have shown
what Kaczynski must surely have known:
that an intern is better
than a bomb in a letter
given the choice to be blown.

Men are always concerned with size
They always try to cover up with lies
But when Titanic came along
It said, "Size matters and ain't wrong."
Hell, now all they DO is rise!

There once was a young boy named Tommy
Who got caught in a giant tsunami
When his mom got horny
After seeing some porny
The poor kid screamed,"No, Mommy!!!"

The old woman who lived in her Shoe
Found a new man she wanted to screw
She said, "Let us Fuck!"

He said, "You must suck!"
Well, this story, is terribly, true....

There once was a horny guy from France,
Who loved to screw frogs in his pants,
He kept going and blowing,
Keeping those frogs from knowing,
He really was in a permanent trance.

There once was a lady from Glee
Who was raped by an ape in a tree.
The result was quite horrid,
all ass and no forehead,
six balls and a purple goatee.

There once was a guy named McSweeney
Who spilled some gin on his weenie
So just to be couth
He added vermouth
And then gave his girl a martini

An elderly roue named Clyde
Took an an eighteen year old as a bride
They took the old lecher
Out on a stretcher
But as he left he was smiling with pride

There was a mortician named Dauphin
Who preferred to sleep in a coffin
It was there that he tried
To make love to his bride
And he did, but not very often.

There once was a girl from Detroit
Who at screwing was considered adroit
She could contract her vagina
To a pinpoint or finer
Or spread it out flat like a plate.

The pleasure of running around nude
Is perceived as being quite rude
Inserting ones pole
Into accessible holes
Isn't just rude but plain lewd

there was a young man from kapits
who planted a whole field of tits
they came up in the fall
red nipples and all
and he leisurely chewed them to bits

there was a young man named jock
who played the bass viol with his cock
with a tremendous erection
he played a selection
from johann sebastian bach

A lassie on one of her larks
Said "it's more fun indoors than in parks
You feel more at ease,
Your ass doesn't freeze,
And strollers don't make snide remarks"

A shapely young lady named Jenna
colored her pubics with henna.
At the beach she was crude
and sunbathed in the nude.
She was promptly invited to dinnah.

There once was a man from Wheeling
His dick with his hand he was feeling
He shot it so high
Up into the sky
He looked up as it dripped from the ceiling

Poante gross and despotic
my tastes are more rich than exotic
I've always adored

making love in a ford
for I am autoerrotic

A bather's clothing was strewed
By a wind that left her quite nude
When a man came along
And unless I am wrong
You expected this line to be lewd

There once was a man from Melbourne
Who really enjoyed watching porn
He whacked with his right
just so he could keep it in sight
Up until his dick was torn

It would watch me when I combed my hair.
It was virile and active, mon cher.
Now it watches (bad news)
As I tie both my shoes.
Oh, when will it end, this nightmare?

There was an old roue named Clyde
Who took an eighteen year old for a bride.
They took the old lecher
Out on a stretcher
But as he left he was smiling with pride.

An ex-submariner named Guido
Had a most tremendous libido.
When he was around women
He just couldn't go swimmin
Because of his gigantic torpedo.

A randy young man from the Cape
Was trying to rape an ape.
The ape said "You fool,
You'll damage your tool
And you're putting my arse out of shape."

There once was a crab named Ickie
Whose shell to the touch was sticky
Off to Heaven he went,
to live in a tent
And there he plays with his dickie.

There once was a man named Sweeney
Who's body parts were kinda teenie
Except when he peed
He smiled with glee
At the size of his rather large weeney.

In the Southland a redneck named Hollis
slept with a snake for his solace.
His children had scales,
and prehensile tails,
and voted for Governor Wallace.

There was a young girl from Dunellen
That the lads in the shipyard called Ellen
In her efforts to please
She spread social disease
From New York to the straights of Magellen

Oh Father, I have a confession.
I have this awful obsession.
The men-of-the-cloth'll
Soon open a brothel.
And I want the condom concession.

There once was a man from St Paul,
Who was born with detachable balls.
When he was bored, he'd remove both his orbs,
And juggle while walking the halls.

There once was a man from Penn Station
Who discovered a brand new sensation.
While fucking his mother

and sucking his brother
he gagged on his sister's menstruation.

There once was a man from china
Who drove a mini minor
He hit a rock and split his cock
And now he's got a vagina

There was a young man from Horsham
Who took out his balls to wash em.
His mother said "Jack,
if you don't put them back
I'll stand on the bastards and squash em."

There was an old man from Calcutta
Who lay down in the gutter.
The sun was so hot
It burnt off his cock
And melted his balls into butter.

There once was a man named Crockett
Who went for a ride in a rocket
The engine went bang
His nuts went clang
And he found his dick in this pocket.

There once was a woman from Neeth
Who circumcised dicks with her teeth
It wasn't for leisure
Or sexual pleasure
It was to get at the cheese underneath

The drugs that we take when we're ailin'
Have alternate names for retailin':
Tylenol's Acetaminophen,
Advil is Ibuprophen
And Viagra is Mycoxafailin.

There was a young gay man from Shank
whose dick got so hot that it shrank
he couldn't believe it
he cut it, relieved it
and sold the next day to a skank

There once was a guy with a joke
whose compensation required a poke
So he shouts to all dames see
who thaught they could tame me
I'm like Ali in the rope-a-dope

There was a young lady so slim
Who had such a very large cwm. **
It wasn't the size
That attracted the flies,
But the crystallized cum on the rim.

I once knew a fair young lass
Her body was made out of glass
You could look down her throat
And from there you could not
Her anatomy right down to her ass

There once was a girl named Karen
That proved to all she was darin'
She jumped on a log
Got humped by a frog
And now all her warts they're a flarin'

A young girl from South Carolina
Place fiddle strings 'cross her vagina
What, with proper sized cocks
once was sex, became Bach's
Tocatta and Fugue in D Minor

An onanist by name of Pickett
Strokes himself while playing cricket...
He squirts on the bails,

It just never fails,
With Pickett, it's sticky, that wicket.

I write while still screwing Annette,
A ravishing, sexy brunette...
"Oh come! Oh please do!"
"I insist, after you..."
The dilemma of sex etiquette!

I shared with a track star my hash
But for sex she demanded hard cash
We settled on price,
I was done in a trice,
She said, "You must sprint in the dash."

Miss Vanderbilt screwed twenty goats
(On their prowess she fervently dotes)
When she was through,
She had a cold brew,
And wrote them all nice thank-you notes.

My horny old aunt, Antoinette,
Inspected me through her lorgnette...
"Your prick's unsurpassed!
I must take a cast!
It'll make such a fine statuette."

Had I shot her in ninety and one,
When I caught her with Steve and his son,
She'd be dead for more years...
I'd be quaffing my beers,
'Cause parole I'd already have won.

A frisky young maid named Jeanette
Married an old baronet...
His prick made her laugh
So with butler and staff
She made up a sexy sextet.

The lord of the manor, Sir Stoat,
Suffered from terminal bloat...
He exploded one day..
They found balls in the hay
And part of his scrote in the moat.

Hill woke up Bill, a cheap shot...
"I' just going to squat on the pot."
"You're going for a pee?
Why alert me?"
"I want you to save me my spot!"

A saggy old matron named Dot
Just sighed as her nipples got hot...
But her tits were adroop
In her clam chowder soup,
So she tied them both up in a knot.

In Shreveport they make a fine stew,
A cultural dish it is true...
They cook up roadkill
With a sprinkling of dill...
It's Chili con Carnage to you!

I'm the very best cook of the group,
I can poach, I can scoop cantaloupe,
I can also roast beef,
Without any grief,
But I'm damned if I'm gonna pee soup!

An alluring but cranky au pair
Was arrested for lethal child care...
The kid was a pain
So she opened his vein,
But swears that he tripped on a stair.

A cannibal chef from Botswana
Said, "Oh it would be sheer Nirvana,
If only I could,

In full babyhood,
Saute an hors d'oeuvre from Montana."

Cogito, Ergo and Sum
Got Rene and his gal a room
When he sat down to cogitate,
She started to masturbate
And invited him up to her womb.

As a king he is fiendishly droll,
The monarch called Merry Old Cole...
His favorite wish
Is to mate with a fish,
So at dinner we never choose sole.

There once was a man from McBride,
Who could fart whenever he tried,
At a contest he blew two thousand and two,
Then shit and was disqualified.

"Oh what's all this ailing, armed Knight?
Loitering paley's not right!
Fuck the sedge and the lake
And that mute bird forsake,
Just tell me about your sad plight."

"I met a neat chick in the Meads...
I set her on one of my steeds..
She made a sweet moan,
Which stiffened my bone,
While I made her a garland of weeds."

"This moaning went on all day long,
While giving me glances sidelong...
'Said she'd relish my root,
Add some honey to boot,
And swore that she'd do me no wrong."

"We finally got to her grotto

(By then on that dew I was blotto)...
She started to bawl,
I could sense a long haul
Ere my prick and her cunt were legato."

"All those sighs and that kissing, a bore!
I just about left through her door,
But she lulled me to sleep
That tease of a creep!
I dreamt she enthralled me, that whore!"

"So you see here a horny young Knight,
Who sojourns with tale all too trite...
Should have focused on twat,
In that damn elfin grot,
And screwed her with all of my might!"

A nudist resort in Benaires
Took a midget in unawares
But he made members weep
For he just couldn't keep
His nose out of private affairs.

There once was a man named McLaren
Whose wife was thought to be barren.
If he had of known
The fault was his own
His youth would of been much more darin'.

There one was a feminist, doris.
Who married a chauvinist, Boris.
He made an improvement,
she gave up the movement.
When she found she had a clitoris.

There was a young man from Calcutta,
Who peeped through a hole in a shutter,
But all he could see,

Was his wife's bare knee,
And the arse of the man who was up her.

I once met a girl called Miss Bish
Who had habits like tropical fish
She would fasten her lips
Close to ones hips
And swallow ones cum in small sips

There once was a clergyman's daughter,
Who detested the pony he bought her,
Till she found that his dong,
was as hard and as long,
As the prayers her father had tought her

She married a fellow named Tony,
Who soon caught her f***ing the pony,
He cried, "What's 'e got,
My dear, that I've not?!"
She sighed, "Just a yard long bologna."

There was an old man from the Nile
Who's behavior was awfully vile
he'd pick at his nose with two of his toes
then belch very loud and smile

There was a young girl named Joan
She went to the dentist's alone
In a fit of depravity
He filled the wrong cavity
And now she nurses the filling at home

Said Lewinsky "All right - I've confessed
Though I'll use 'Bill's defence' - it's the best
I will say 'I was silly
to play with Bill's willy'
- but I sucked and I didn't ingest"

A belly dancer called Wendy
Aspired to being modern and trendy
To a chorus of yells
She removed all seven veils
Driving her fans to a frenzy

There was a young man from the cape,
Who tried to make love to an ape.
The ape said "Stop it you fool,
You're bending your tool,
And pushing my arse out of shape."

There was an old man called Col,
who thought every hole was a goal
He would fill any gap
and shoot up his sap
until his dick got stuck in a mole

What's the deal with this toilet-seat crap?
If we don't put it up, there's a flap.
Leave it up, and we get,
A new lecture yet.
Either way, we'll be in for a rap.

There once was a Scot named McAmeter,
Whose tool had prodigious diameter.
But it wasn't his size
That gave girls their surprise...
'Twas his rhythm--iambic pentameter.

If you crossed a young intern, Lewinsky,
With a man by the name of Kaczynski,
Then the blow jobs you'd get
Would be dynamite! Yet,
You might end up without a fore-skin-ski!

There once was a man named Mike.
Who sported an enormous spike.
His girl said with a grin,

"It's hard to get in,
But that's the size that I like"

There once was a woman from Anheiser,
Who swore that no man could surprise her.
But Pabst took a chance,
Found a Schlitz in her pants,
and now she is sadder Budweiser!

There once was a woman from Hoboken,
Who claimed her cherry was broken,
From riding a bike,
On a cobblestone pike,
But it really was broken from pokin'!

There once was a woman from Arden,
Who sucked off her man in a garden.
He said, "My dear Flo,
Where does all that stuff go?"
And she said, "MMMMMNG, I beg your pardon?"

There once was a milkman named Schwartz,
Whose cock was all covered with warts.
But women would play,
with his dick anyway,
'cause good ol' Schwartz came in quarts.

There was this belle from Bangalore,
so sweet and pure when she was four,
When she was sixteen of age,
She went to Maharani's college,
And now everyone thought She was a Whore!

A young violinist from Reo,
Was seducing a woman named Cleo;
As she took down her panties,
She said "No 'andantes',
I want this 'allegro con brio'.

I think my teacher is smart
He has such a wonderful heart
He said with a grin
As it rumbled within
That smell in the air is a fart

one night wile fucking his wife Dr Zuck
in his ears got his wife's nipples stuck
with his thumb up her bum
he could hear himself come
thus inventing the TELEPHONE FUCK!

A lonely old man at the zoo
Seemed to have nothing better to do
Than to eye the Giraffe,
But unbeknownst to the staff,
He was secretly balling the gnu.

There once was a lass from Gibralter
Whose purity a young man did alter
But just ere she came
He reddened with shame,
For the strength of his manhood did falter.

There was a young woman from Madrass
who I took for a walk in the grass
With fingers so slim..I fingered her quim
Till it foamed like a bottle of bass.

There was a young woman from west Houghton
Who had a long Tit and a short one
So to make up for that
she had a lopsided twat
and a fart like a five hundred Noughton.

there once was a fellow named clyde
but his girth was so far from wide
when he expelled a gas

he fell through his ass
hanging there till he strangled and died

There once was a vicar from Kew,
Who preached with his vestments askew,
A woman named Morgan,
Caught sight of his organ,
And promptly passed out in her pew

There once was a young man from Brighton,
Who remarked to his woman, "My, you're a tight one."
She said, "Upon my soul,
You're in the wrong hole,
There's plenty of room in the right one!"

There once was a man from Goshum
who took off his balls to wash 'em
His wife said Jack
if you don't put 'em back
I'll put 'em in the wringer and squash'em.

Thus spake Madame du Berry
"I fear my son is a fairy
the problem you see
is he sits down to pee.
Yet he stands when I bathe the canary."

The new cinematic emporium
was more than a super sensorium
it was highly effectual
as a heterosexual
mutual masturbatorium

yesterday I called up my mother
I said, "dear mom there is another,
she gives good head too
and she's younger than you
why don't you date my dear brother"

I asked an old crofter on Skye,
what he did in the winter -- and why.
I received an offensive,
obscene, comprehensive,
and monosyllabic reply!!

There was an ol' Gal with gray hair.
Who gave all the young fellers' a stare.
She'd offer them treats,
of her wrinkled up meat.
But when you're young & horny, who cared?

A fountain of passion they found.
Among her mountains of aged ground round.
So sweet be a tart.
But offers nothing more than a fart!
Five fingered romance will always be found.

There once was a man named Magruder
who met a girl in the nude, and he wooed her.
She thought it was crude
to be wooed in the nude,
but Magreuder was shrewd and he screwed her.

It was 4 a.m. when I finally hit the hay
For I had been studying all day.
But my brain turned to mush
So I bought a case of Busch
And got a hangover that wont go away.

When a horny old man fell asleep in the sun,
the zipper on his fly somehow came undone,
He awoke with a smile,
Said, "My gosh, a sundial,
And it's not a quarter past one.

The once were two men in black suits
who had trouble controlling their poots
At lunch one finally said

As the other nodded his head
We should switch now from beans to fruits

There once was a woman from Latch
Who jacked herself with a match
She got so excited
Then damn thing ignited
And burnt all the hair off her snatch

There once was a man from Cape Horn
He wished he had never been born
He Shouldn¦t have been
If his father had seen
That the end of his french letter was torn

There once was a man from Istanbul
Who had some red marks on his tool
He went to the doc
Who looked at his cock
And said "Wipe off the lipstick you fool."

There once was a president named Bill
Who had quite a thrill
As an intern named Monica
Played like a harmonica
All over his Capitol Hill

There was once man named Penn
who said "Let us do it again,
And again and again
and again and again
and again and again and again!"

There once was a lady from Exeter
and the men in the street craned their necks at her
One day to be rude,
she reclined in the nude
while her parrot, a pervert, took pecks at her.

There once was a man named Vance,
who was well endowed in his pants,
when the ladies caught view,
they knew it was true,
and they had been put in a trance

I knew a young lady named Claire,
Who possessed a magnificent pair,
Or that's what I thought,
Till I saw one get caught,
On a thorn and begin losing air.

There was a young woman from Leeds,
who swallowed a packet of seeds,
in less than an hour,
her tits were all flowers,
and her arse was covered in weeds.

To her beau, said the willing young lass,
"There's only one thing that I ask:
When I am bent over
and you're in me like Rover,
please don't set your drink on my ass!".

'Twas said that a SEFE named Hal
used a checklist for mounting his gal
he'd brief her, advise her,
debrief and surprise her,
then give her an oral eval

There once was a president named Bill
Who gave all the interns a thrill,
One day he did spew,
On a dress that was blue
And now his presidency is nill

There once was a man from Bombay
Who ate gallons of beans ev'ry day

He farted so loud,
He attracted a crowd
But the smell made them all run away.

There was once a guy from New Dheli
Who could fit fifty girls on his belly
When asked how they fit,
He said, "Tit to tit
and by gum, don't they make my nuts jelly."

We once knew a girl from Lake Forest
Who had a GIGANTIC clitoris
Now this may sound dumb,
But whenever we'd come
She'd already been there before us.

There once was a knight who defiled
a young maiden's virtue and pride.
But let it be known
that is you rape someone
You'll get a hot chick as your bride.

There once was a girl called Billie,
Who liked to suck Troy's willy,
When Lisa told her off
Bill' gave an almighty cough...
Then she kicked Lisa's slats in the filly.

There once was a fellow named Ernie
who's profession was pushing a gurney
from hospital room
to the morgue and its gloom
was this Ernie's favorite journey.

Honestly it's not water I'm duckin'
while gallons of beer I may suck in
the source of my fear
is perfectly clear
I don't drink that which fish like to fuck in.

Frisky in bed as a colt
Was youthful ace golfer Tom Bolt
But after his lay up
He'd come in a small cup
Driving his wife to revolt.

I like just a tad of asymmetry
It adds to a breast a sublimity...
A little more heft
Right tit or left
I enjoy with bemused equanimity.

She wasn't too bold, not too willing
And she did stare a lot at the ceiling...
But once with this rogue
She put down her vogue
And said, "That was mod'rately thrilling."

A gorgeous young girl, Dominique
Had a pussy like milky Lalique,
'Twas lovely and pale,
That creamy soft vale,
And displayed at a glazier's boutique.

A man with a very long foreskin
Said, "Doc, I'll be needing some more skin..."
So they did a quick graft
'Pon the head of his shaft,
He's now in the Book of Folklore Skins.

There was a chicken farmer from Hay,
Who found his hens wouldn't lay;
The trouble was Brewster,
His champion rooster;
You see, Brewster the rooster was gay!

There once was a man named Chang,
Who had an incredible wang.

He was tallented too.
For all night he could screw.
And the girls his praises all sang.

Up in Redmond sits wealthy Bill Gates,
Who is richer than all fifty states.
Janet Reno is jealous
And overly zealous,
'Cause Bill never asked her for dates.

There once was a young man named Justin
Who got caught by his mom when lustin'
While cybering with "hedgethorn"
and looking at hardcore porn
And his daddy gave him a good bustin'

There once was a U.S.Marine
Whose manners were slightly unclean
He liked to eat jizz
Both other's and his
When served in a hot soup tourene

There once was a man from Seattle
whose hobby was sucking off cattle
'til a holstein named Keith
blew a load through his teeth
and put 'im right back in the saddle

There was an old Irish mick
whose cum was exceedingly thick
He could squeeze it out
And spray it about
But it stuck to the end of his dick.

There was a man from Capri
Who tried to piss over a tree
The tree was too high
And it fell in his eye
And now the poor bugger can't see.

There was a young whore from Kilkenny,
Who charged two fucks for a penny,
For half of that sum,
You could bugger her bum,
An economy practised by many

There once was a man named Harry
Whose balls were so very scary
When he would take a piss
He would moan and hiss
Because it was too heavy to carry.

There was a guy I wanted to be mine
so I told him "You be six and I'll be nine"
"we can have fun and then a Lay
Yes, I'm talking to you Joe Day!"
Then he said "Damn you're fine!!!"

There was a young lady named Hilda
who went on a date with a builder -
he asked if he should -
she said that he could -
so he did, and very near killed her!

A policeman from near Clapham Junction
had a penis that just would not function;
for his whole married life,
he deluded his wife,
with some snot on the end of his truncheon

There was a young man from Calcutta
who peeked through a hole in a shutter,
all he could see
was a prostitute's knee,
and the bum of the chap that was up her!

There was a young lady from Ongar
who was shagged in the sea, by a conger,

her girl friend from Deal,
asked "how did it feel?"
she said "nice - like a man - only longer!"

A lighthouse keeper called Crighton
took to seeing a lady from Brighton,
but ships ran aground,
and sailors were drowned,
as she wouldn't have sex with the light on

There once was a whore on the dock
From dusk until dawn she sucked cock
'Til one day it's said
She gave so much head
She exploded and whitewashed the block

When her daughter got married in Bicester,
Her mother remarked as she kissed her,
"That fellow you've won,
Is sure to be fun,
Since tea he's fucked me and your sister."

There once was a lass from Nantucket,
Who went to the moon in a bucket.
When she got there,
they asked for her fare.
So she stuck out her tit and said, "Suck it!"

There was a young girl of Nant FFrancon
Whose chastity no-one would bank on
She rogered Prince Andy
And Tony - but Mandy
Was one guy she just drew a blank on.

There once was a lady from France
Who kept a baboon in her pants
half the people who saw
couldn't help but guffaw
but the rest of them asked her to dance.

There once was a man from Far Rockaway
That could smell a piece-of-ass about a block away
One night he got a whif,
but she had the "siff"
And now it's eating his cock-a-way

I sat with the Dutchess at tea
She said "Do you fart when you pee?"
I said with some whit
"Do you belch when you shit?"
And thought it was one up for me!

The latest word from the dean,
Regarding the teaching machine,
Is that Oedipus Rex,
Could have learned about sex,
Alone without bothering the queen.

One morning Mahatama Gandhi
Had a hard on, and it was a dandy!
He said to his aide,
"Please bring me a maid,
Or a goat, or whatever is handy!"

there once was a guy at a mall
who thought he was tough shit and all
he thought he was slick
when he whipped out his dick
but girls laughed cause his dick was too small

There once was a man from Montanna
Who said he could play the pianna
His finger slipped
His zipper ripped
And out came a hairy banana

There once was a man named Moran
A bad lover who drove a van

He'd take a girl home
Then leave her alone
Said he,"I'm in love with my hand!"

There once was a lady named Mable,
whose ass was as big as a table.
"Never you mind."
said a frind of mine.
She's ready, willing, and able.

This girl liked to swim everyday
She always said "its like play"
but when she removed
her clothing she proved
her body was not for display

There once was a girl named Jill
She had a licence to kill
Instead of shopping,
she went head-bopping
And now she has to pay the death bill.

There once was a knight named sir Lancelot,
Whom the people all looked at askance a lot
For whenever he'd pass,
A delectable lass,
The front of his pants would advance a lot.,

There was a young gal from Iconium,
Who's dildo was made from Plutonium,
But when deep in her ass,
It reached critical mass,
There WAS a young gal from Iconium.

There was a man from Tamil Nadu
Who knew a lot of Jadoo
Once during a trick
He lost his prick
And now he is a sadoo

Leo and scott played tennis,
in a quiet little town of Venice.
They used special balls,
that used to be Paul's,
and now Paul feels quite tremendos.

There once was a boy named Ian,
and his entire reason for bein'.
Was to stand in the stall,
holdin' it all,
and enjoying himself while peein'.

There was an old bishop from Bavery
Addicted to deeds obscene and unsavory
Amidst rumbles and howls
He deflowered young owls
In the depths of his underground aviary

In the White House there roams a liberal named Bill
Whose election wrought repubicans ill will
But when Bill made a mess
On the intern's new dress
Republicans sought impeachment with zeal

The word spread like fire through our land
of an affair that got perversly out of hand
While Hillary was playing dumb
Her husband was getting gummed
In the halls of our great high command

Now while Bill did his job without care
The nation went ga ga over the Capitol pair
And it wasn't till later
After he lied we found he did cater
To the tempations of the girl with big hair

There once was a villian most feared,
Who tied a lass to a train track then leered,

But he tied her up wrong-ways,
Not cross-ways but long-ways,
And a forty car train disappeared!

There once was a girl from Vancouver
Whose mouth had the strength of a Hoover;
When she turned it on high,
A week would pass by,
Before anyone could remove her.

I had an ex-roommate Pierre,
Who once fell asleep in my chair.
I pulled out my unit,
Proceded to tune it,
And fired a load in his hair.

A lady who "hooks" for a living,
Had no chest, so her profits were thinning.
She got her boobs stuffed,
Now they're quite big enough,
To give a whole new lift to "Thanksgiving"!

There once was a girl named Teddi,
Whose hair was stuck together like spaghetti.
It was covered with Cheese,
All the way to her knees,
So you had to part her legs with a machete.

There was a young lass named flower,
Who lived on a hill in a tower.
She hosted a show,
And we all got to go
Watch her dance around in the shower.

There once was a girl called Rene
Who had two brothers, both were gay
If you give 'em a buck
they'll give you a fuck
Then will happily walk away

Old Bill's wife was a nasty old hag
Each damn day she was on the rag!
He made her some strap-ons
Out of super thick tampons
But she still won't use a douche bag!

No longer does Bill try to please her
Instead, he puts turds in the freezer
A condom for a wrapper
They go back up his crapper
And he cums like no other old geezer

Her fancy he will no longer tickle
He cuddles only with his crap-sickle
What that crazy old coot
Pushes up his poop-chute
Makes a boner of his wrinkled ol' pickle

Left his wife to be a mountaineer
Just sits in the snow and drinks Bush beer
He needs no ice box
To make his turd-cocks
And once in a while, he fucks reindeer

And if he gets lonely and feels low
He cops a squat to make a dildo
Thinks of bloody tampons
Laces up his crampons
And is glad he left that bloody ho!

There once was a lady named McBagg
And to all the ladies she did brag
"My breasts are sizeable,
And easily recognizeable
I rarely have to wear a name tag."

There once was a young man named Gus
Who for animals had a great lust

He buggered and owl,
two dogs, and a fowl
And a little green lizard that Bust

There once was a man from Nantucket
Who was fucking a pig in a bucket
The pig said with a grunt
"That's my ass, not my cunt.
Come around to the front and I'll suck it."

Said the Indian Chief to the Totem
"My wife's breasts are so large she can float 'em!
All the tribe members stare.
It's unbearable. There...
...fore, I bought her a bag for to tote 'em!

A man back from Alpha Centauri
Tells a perfectly horrible story
Their women have teeth
Both above and beneath
And whatever goes in comes out gory!

A turd dropped by Sister Ecclesia
Reached from Key West to Southern Rhodesia
The cause of this dump
Was a three-foot-square lump
Of Ex-Lax laced with Milk of Magnesia

As to rape mused Joe Blow in Cell 9
I'll take any cunt-hole for mine
Dogs,sheep,mares or squirrels
Or if nothing else girls
As long as it stinks man it's fine!

There once was a man from Dakota
Who didn't pay a whore what he owed her
She jumped out of bed,
her c-nt flaming red
And pissed in his whiskey and soda

There was a young mister from Blister
Who knocked up his gal as he kissed her.
But he couldn't afford
A new baby on board,
So from then on he just had to fist her.

There was a lady in Cincinatti
by the sweet name of Patty
once a man had her
and so roughly did buggar
that she is now plain batty.

there once was a sad man from Leeds
who lay every night alone under the sheets
he spend his sorry life
without the company of a wife
and he had to fullfill his own needs

Big Brother Blucher of Brest
Insistently sinned by incest.
He buggered his brother,
And mounted his mother,
But insisted his sister was best.

There once was a couple from Arburiswith
That made love with the things that they kissed with
But as they grew older
They got even bolder
And made love with the things that they pissed with

There was a young man from Gosham,
Who took out his bollocks to wash em,
His wife said Jack, if you don't put them back
I'l stand on the bastards and squash em.

There once lived a man in DC
Who'd been shut off by his wife Hillary
He refused to confess

But the proof's on the dress
So quit lying to us on T.V.

A new farmer's helper named Kull
accidently was milking a bull
the farmer said "Boy, you're dumb
you milked the wrong one!"
said the boy "But me whole buckets full!"

When his daddy told young Willie Plum
How and where new babies come from
Willie sneered, "For two years,
I've been humpin' Sue Meers,
And she's had no kid papa you dumb.

there once was a gay horny guy
who wanted to screw a fly
he looked at a girl
and started to hurl
and thought "if i had to screw a girl i'd die"

There once was a man from seattle
he loved having sex with his cattle
one day he got hurt
when his twang hit the dirt
and now he straps into the saddle

Bradley has a thong
His hoo-hoo's not very long
It attracts women with stubble
Just like Barney Rubble
With whom he stays with all night long

Bradley's thong is teeney
It almost exposes his weenie
But he's not very big
'bout the size of a twig
There's no lump in his bikini

Joey likes Brad's thong
He says it excites his schlong
Together they wrestle
It gives them a special
Feeling down by their wongs.

There was a lady from Seattle
Who got off blowing off cattle
Until a bull from the south
Shot a load in her mouth
that made both of her ovaries rattle

There was a young wife from Vancouver
who had a mouth like a Hoover
her husband, in bed,
was no fun, she said,
he just didn't like that maneuver

There once was a girl named Savanna
whose coochie was big as Montana
she opens her legs
and softly she begs
stick in that massive banana

While Titian was mixing rose madder
His model ascended a ladder
Her position to Titian
Suggested coition
So he climbed up the ladder and had her

There once was a priest from Siberia
Who motives were very ulterior
He done to a nun
What he shouldn't have done
And now she's Mother Superior.

there once was a man from Seatle
who got his dick cut off in a battle
he said "Hollly Shit'

it looks like a clit"
and now he whacks off with a paddle

Old King Billy had a ten foot Willy,
And he showed it to the lady next door,
She though it was a snake,
So she hit it with a rake,
And now it's only five foot four.

A dignified lady of York,
tried to eat krap on a fork
Her son cried "you goon"
"you eat shit with a spoon
it's pork ya eat with a fork!"

Slick Willy gets away with a lot
He's had many a lass in his cot.
His polls keep ascending,
though lawsuits are pending
Yet his record shows nary a blot.

Bill Clinton's a puzzling soul
Getting laid seems to be his main goal.
He'll pick out a sow
and proceed to drop trou.
Popularity shoots up his poll.

A tuna sat next to his brother,
Their Dad looked from one to the other,
"boys" he said "listen,
two things smell like fish'n
both of those things are your mother"

Poor Rushy had a budding romance,
But his thingie went zingy at a glance.
A bit to much tilt,
and up came his kilt,
And she laughed at his tiny love lance.

The new wife was the cheating slut kind.
But soon she was busted she'd find,
With pics at the wedding.
The best man in her bedding.
Doing more than pinching her hind.

there was a young laddie named Jock.
who had a most horrible shock.
He once took a shit
in a leaf covered pit
and the crap sprung a trap on his cock

There was a young man named Keith,
who liked to be fondeled beneeth.
When she used her lips,
he wiggled his hips,
but not when the bitch used her teeth.

There once was a rooster from Tarmer
Who thought he was quite the charmer
Until, by the shed
He lost his proud head
To the rusty red axe of the farmer.

There once was a man named Rex
Who had a problem getting sex
He went for some rum
Instead it was cum
Today other guys he connects

A lovely, young lady named Lola,
Had a no elastic left in her cola,
The poor little lass,
Shot a turd out her ass..
Like it was lubed up with Crisco Canola!!!

There was a young man from Taiwan
Who ordered one ton of wonton
His perversion prooved heinous

For he whipped out his penis
And tied one Taiwon wonton on!

There once was a girl named Lewinsky
Who married Carol Linskey
They went to Bill's house
Got a stain on their blouse
Now Ms.Lewinsky is stinky!

There was a young woman from the Heath
Who circumsized men with her teeth
It's all very funny
'cos it wasn't for money
But for the cheese that she found underneath!

There was a young copper from the junction
Whose penis just wouldn't function
He fooled his poor wife
For the whole of her life
With some snot on the end of his truncheon.

There was a young plumber from Lee,
who was plumbing his girl with glee,
she said stop your plumbing,
I think someones coming,
said the plumber still plumbing "its me!"

There was a policeman from Andover Junction
Whose organ just wouldn't function
Throughout his married life
He deceived his poor wife
With a Wiltshire Constabulary truncheon!!

My name is Danielle Bissonette
And I hope that you don't soon forget
For if you're mistaken
Your butt will be achin'
And that aint a hollow threat!

There once was a man from Brighton
who said to his girl "You're a tight one!"
she said "Pon my soul,
You're in the wrong hole!,
Theres plenty of room in the right one!"

I never wrote a limerick with orgy in it
Seems I'd have trouble beginnin' it
On the other hand my rhymes
At least some of the times
Have lotsa fun and sin in it!

Greg was a wee lad from Belfast
Whose bombs, they made quite the blast
He said just today
"If I joined the I.R.A.
British rule would be a thing of the past!"

Legend tells of a knight named Sir Hunt,
Whose cock performed an incredible stunt.
His versatile spout,
Could be turned inside-out,
And thereafter be used as a cunt.

There once was a girl named Reshan,
who everyone thought was a man.
her big healthy breasts,
bounced off my chest,
and went right up into the fan.

There once was a man named Jack
He kept his dick stuck up his crack
When he sat down
He went to town
On his little friend he named Zack

Busty Sue was thrilled to bits,
To be staying at the London Ritz,
As the clerk checked her in,

He gave her a sly grin,
As he surreptitiously checked out her tits.

A morose young monk from Siberia,
Daily grew drearier and drearier,
Until with a yell,
He burst from his cell,
And buggered the Mother Superior.

A remarkable race are the Persians,
With so many sexual diversions,
They make love all day,
In the regular way,
And save up the night for perversions.

A Hollywood actress of note
Bought an expensive fur coat
They said it was mink
But it wasn't, I think
from the smell it was Angorra goat

There once was a man named Fred,
His wife wouldn't give any head,
so he jumped on his horse,
to get a divorce,
but jumped off and jacked off instead.

A sousaphone tooter named Bjorn
Was in love with his bright, shiny horn.
He'd lovingly hold her
Astride of his shoulder
She was tongued, she was fingered and worn.

As piccolo players all know
A piccolo's quite fun to blow.
You get lots of thrills
From those triple-tongue trills.
And your horn's a good fake prickle, OH!

A percussionist out of St. Peete
Had a drum set made only of "Treet"
He said, with a pause
When asked "Why?" "Because
I like sitting 'round beating my meat."

A girl with a shiny trombone
Is never, no never alone.
She's famous with guys
When they realize
She uses lip, slide and tongue to find tone.

There once was a fellow called Hough
His Mother's obscenely Rough
She's not very choosy
Some say she's a floozy
And not a nice sight in the buff

There once was a girl from Illinois
Who liked to climb trees with the boys
Tho she did't flirt
They'd look up her skirt
With holes in their pockets for toys

There was a poor girl on the street,
In trash cans found leftovers to eat.
She thought she had garbage stew.
That tasted like a horse's doo,
Yet demands it tasted quite sweet.

After Joe shot his wad into Ann,
She thought she'd douched out in the can.
But she missed by a myriad
And skipped her next period,
And old Joe's on his way to Japan.

There once was a Prez from Little Rock
Who wanted this young thing on his little cock
So he says of her "Dear Monica"

"Come and play my Harmonica"
Then to Tripp she gave a little talk

A Draughtsman residing in Poole
Was possessed of a singular tool.
Said he, matter-of-factly,
It's twelve inches exactly
But I don't use it much as a rule.

There was a young man from New Castle,
Who recieved a brown paper parcel.
In it was shit,
And on it was writ,
A message to you from my asshole.

We once knew a girl from Lake Forest
blessed with a gigantic clitoris.
though this might sound dumb
whenever we'd come,
She'd already been there before us.

There was a young lady from chester,
who stood in a field and undressed her,
a copper came by,
and said what a beauty,
it took 24 hours to arrest her.

There once was a man named Starky
Who had an affair with a Donkey
The result of his Sins
Were Quadruplets not Twins
One Black, One White and Two Khakhi

There once was a lady from Exeter,
And all the young men threw their sex at her.
So just to be crude,
She laid in the nude,
While her parrot, a pervert, took pecks at her.

There once was a guy who passed gas
Who did IT right there in the grass
'Till one night in bed
His boyfriend, Ted said
"Tonight it goes right up the ass!"

There once was a dentist named Sloan
Who started his practice with a Loan
When he succumbed to Proclivity
And filled the wrong Cavity
What he heard was a moan, not a Groan

There once was this teen-aged Dork
Who was always pounding his Pork
After he got his first Piece
From his sixteen year old Niece
The next thing that came was the Stork

Out west lived a cowboy named Rick
Who, with a lariat, could perform any trick
It was out behind the saloon
One sunny day in June
That he lassoed a bull by the dick

There once was a man named Odom
Whose balls were too big for his scrotom
Though it was relief that he sought
It all went for naught
Cause he didn't know how to unloadem

There once was a man named Sweeny
whose wife was a terrible meany
The hatch on her snatch
Had a catch that would latch
And she could only get fucked by Houdini

A evil young woman from Malta
Killed her poor aunt with a halter
She said "I won't bury her"

"She'll do for my terrier"
"She should keep for a month, if I salt her"

there once was a boy who lived in the hay,
all he thought about was foreplay.
the sex was great,
but not his fate.
so he decides to go gay.

There was a guy from Nantucket
he told his wife to suck it
when he didn't cum
she told him he was dumb
and hit him upside the head with a bucket

There once was a guy with great pecs
his obssesion was with sex
he liked it up the ass
with girls who had no class
who called him T-rex

There once was a boy named Phil
whose girlfriend forgot to take the pill
they went to bed
he got more than head
when they went up the hill

There once was a nun from Siberia
Who was born with a virgin interior
Until a young monk
Jumped into her bunk
And now she's a mother superior!

There once was a man named Vic
Who pleasured himself with a stick
He once got it stuck
and said "what the fuck?"
and now there's no room for a prick!

there was an old man from New Castle
who wrapped up a shit in a parcel
he sent it by train
with a note to explain
that it came from his grandmothers asshole

There once was a girl named Becs
Who liked to have lots of sex
With the guys in a line
She'd take them one at a time
And when she was done she'd yell "next!"

Willy had a problem with his plumbing,
He kept spontaneously coming,
At an interview one day,
He came during it part way,
And said "Well that put me out of the running."

I know of a Scotsman, a Jock,
Who's got the most extraordinary cock,
He's lucky you see,
'Cause it's shaped like a key,
And with it he can pick any girls' lock.

There lived an old man by the bay
Who wanted to find a good lay
He wooed a young lass
With a tight little ass
He just didn't know he'd have to pay.

There was a young lady named Myrtle,
Who amused herself with a sea-turtle.
And what was phenomenal,
A swelling abdominal,
Revealed that the turtle....was fertil!

After reading your limerick's tonight on St. Patrick's Day,
I got inspired and wrote this one for my Irish lady friend.

I love madly a faire maiden named Lynne
Her eyes are as green as Irish gin
When the liquor's within her
I like to lick her and grin
"Cause she tastes like a tangy gin fizz

There once was a wonderful wizard
who had a great pain in his gizzard
So he ate wind and snow
at 50 below
and farted a forty day blizzard.

There once was a man from down under
When he fucked it sounded like thunder
He said "Hey there Mate!
Why masterbate?
Oh! Look at your dick, it's no wonder!"

There was a lad from Montana
Who had a wife named Hannah
He could not get wood
So impatient he stood
With a Vaseline enhanced banana!

There once was a man from Seoul
His pecker he always did pull
He cut a hole in his pocket
To stroke on his rocket
So he never got caught in school!

There was an old codger from Crockett
Who stuck his dick in a socket.
"I hope I don't burn it
Or otherwise ruin it
Cause I'll miss it like crazy, Goldurnit!!"

There was a man named Bertrand
Who was suffering from anxiety he could not stand.
He went to bed, that night,

With a love problem, extremely uptight,
But woke up with a solution in hand.

There was a young boy from Caboo,
Who had trouble tying his shoe.
He said to his ox
"I'll just walk in my socks".
Now all of his freind do that, too!

A young man of unknown idenity
Went swimming in our vicinity
Because he was nuda
A blind baracuda
Ran off with his masculinity.

There was a young lad named Bart
Who caused a stink from the start
Said a tithering twit
I think surely he's shit
Tho he said it was only a fart.

There once was a president named Bill.
Who never was able to get his fill.
He met a bitch
who would scratch his itch
and now the whole world is ill.

There was a magician from Purdue
He thought he was good but was new
he tried a vanishing trick
and lost his prick
and now he's become a 'saadhu'

There was a young lady from Exeter,
So lovely that men craned their necks at her.
One was even so brave
As to take out and wave
The distinguishing sign of his sex at her.

There was a young lady named Monica
She just had a terrible Hannukah
For revealing her versions
Of White House perversions
On Mem'rex, and Maxell and Konica.

There was a young girl named Hazel
Who had hair growing out of her navel
The sissors she got
cut out a neat spot
now her belly is up for appraisal

There was a young man, an engineer,
Who liked to drink way too much beer,
One night whilst blind drunk,
He was last seen with a monk,
And now all of his friends think he's queer.

There was a young lady named Banker,
Who slept while the ship lay at anchor.
She awoke in dismay,
When she heard the mate say,
"Hoist up the top sheet and spanker."

There once was a crack head that was mean,
He didn't pay me, so I broke his spleen.
He had to stop doing crack,
Got up off his back.
Got a job and is now a dope-fiend.

There once was a man from Nantucket
Who kept all his cash in a bucket
His wife named Fran
Ran away with a man
"Oh said the man "Just Fuck it"

A lovely young lady at sea
complained that it hurt her to pee.
Said the burly First Mate:

"That accounts for the fate
of the cook and the captain and me."

The sex of an astroid vermin
Is exceedingly hard to determine
So galactic patrol
Simply fucks any hole
That will possibly let all the sperm in

There was a young spaceman from Venus
Who had a prodigious penis
Cried his girlfriend alas
It just came out my ass
And there is still 15 inches between us.

A horny young blond from Vancouver
Liposuctioned herself with a hoover
Despite the seduction
Achieved by the suction
Was generally thought to improve 'er

there was a man from cuba
who stuck his dick in a tuba
His newly wed bride
blew on the other side
and his dick flew off to Aruba

There once was a young girl named Charlotte
Who made extra cash as a harlot
She screwed a producer
Who tried to seduce her
And now shes a Hollywood Starlet!

There once was a man named Ron Rice
whose privates were ravaged by lice
he scrubbed and he scratched,
but still more were hatched
if you've had it, you know it aint nice

In Las Vegas a maiden named Carol
Was arrested for wearing a barrel.
She'd not drawn the joker
While playing strip poker
And lost all her other apparel.

I once met a beautiful Persian
A shy one who needed coercion
So I gave her a smile
And she thought for a while
Then allowed me to make an insertion.

I once knew two sisters whose breasts
They exposed to their thunderstruck guests
A policeman was called
And the young chap, enthralled
Ogled, but made no arrests.

From deep in the crypt at St Giles
Came a scream which resounded for miles.
Said the Vicar "Good gracious!
Has Father Ignatius,
Forgotten the Bishop has piles!?!?

There once was a man named Bill
Who had a loyal wife named Hill
He played harmonica
Made love to Monica
And now he's in for the kill!

There once was a boy named Mark
Who liked to have sexual fun in the dark
One day his dad walked through the door
And Mark's vibrater fell to the floor
So now Mark vibrates his ass in the park.

There once was a gal from Racine
Who was bound to do something obscene
So she stripped herself bare

And sold everyone a share
At Merril-Lynch, Pierce-Fenner and Beane

A cardiac patient named Fred
Made a limerick up in his head.
He didn't have time.
To right down all the lines....

A limerick writer named Ryan
Made up limericks all the time.
The thoughts that he had
Were usually bad,
But this one has no dirty lines.

On the Dark side there was a Darth Vader.
Who said, "Luke, I am your father, your creator."
One more secret's this.
Princess Laya's your sis.
Luke thought, "Damn, and I wanted to lay her."

There once was a man named Bob,
Who wanted an ass for his knob.
He bought an old whore,
Entered the backdoor.
He wishes she wiped, that slob.

There once was a fresh seafood cook,
Whose penis resembled a hook.
He wasn't much of an angler,
But he snagged fish with dangler,
'Till he lost his rod in a brook.

A young exhibitionist called Rex,
Finds public places most fun to have sex,
So he did his girl Tina,
At Wembley Arena,
And now they're thrilling crowds at the G-MEX.

There once was a preacher's daughter
who resented the pony he bought her
till she found that it's dong
was as hard and as long
as the prayers her father had taught her

She married a man named Tony
who soon caught her fucking the pony
he cried "What's it got
My dear, that I've not?"
and she sighed, "just a yard-long bologna."

there was a young girl from Sofia,
who succumbed to her lover's desire.
she said, "it's a sin,
but now that it's in,
could you shove it a few inches higher?"

There once was a woman from China,
Who went to sea on a liner,
She sliped on the deck,
And twisted her neck,
And now can see up her vagina.

I went to a bar called "Rick's"
And took home in my car two chicks
I pulled off my pants
They threw me a glance
And said "We've seen much larger dicks!"

I had a dog named Lucky
Who was a horny fucky
One day he found
The neighbor's hound
And got his sausage stucky!

There was a young whore from Trotten
Whose tastes were pervertedly rotten
She cared not for steaks

Or pastries and cakes
But lived upon penis au gratin.

There was a young lady from Bath,
Who loved to make love in the grass,
"It is better than a bed",
"I can rest my head",
"And I love how it tickles my ass".

While playing a good round of golf
I got hit and my pecker fell off
But I still have a stub
And although its no sub
I can now use my dick as a club

There was an old man from Bangkok,
Whose dick was as hard as a rock,
The day came, he died,
And they say its no lie,
That the man died, but his hard on did not

Whitey was a kid who had a knack
for running around the high school track
but one day his lance
fell out of his pants
now he is called tic tac

once upon a starry night
a kid named whitey said with might
i am the biggest, best, and long
just look at my gorgeous dong
and hollie laughed and said "yeah right"

There once was an actor from Wales
His beauty was hard to detail
His talent was none
His career soon done
When the papers said "he's not male!"

There once was a boy named bob
Who one day screwed his door knob
it got stuck in his ass
but it felt better than his bass
and now he can't do his pimp job

There once was a girl from Nantuket
Who rode to Hell in a bucket,
But when she got there
They asked for her fare,
So she pulled up her skirt and said, "Fuck it!"

There once was a man from L.A.
Who sucked himself off everyday
He didn't like muff,
It was not deep enough
So everyone thought he was gay.

A possessive young fellow from Maine,
tied his wife to the sink with a chain.
The chain soon was rusted,
the husband got busted,
And communal showers mean pain

There was once a man from Oostend
Whose wife caught him fucking her friend
He said it's no use my duck
Interrupting this fuck
For Im damned if I draw til I spend!

A juggling cat named Pierre
Liked to walk with his tail in the air.
When the girl cats passed by
They said, "My, oh my--
What a nice set of balls you have there!"

Cruel Julie did have in her hands
An abundance of strong rubber bands
She shot one at me

And hit my wee wee
And injured my organs and glands

there once was a bitch named sherry
she wished a guy she could marry
since her daughter got some
and she could get none
she looked for a goat named larry

There once was a women from mass
Who had a very large ass
when asked does it shake
she said with a quake
No, but it does pass some gas

There was a young man from Pool
Who had concentric rings 'round his tool
He went to a clinic
The doctor--a cynic--
Said "wash it, it's lipstick, you fool!"

I knew a man from Bangladesh
Who liked his females clothed in mesh
Any color or shape,
Just so he could gape
At the supple feminine flesh.

A very great man from Taiwan
Was incurably given to yawn.
He thought it quite banal
and unbelievably anal
When girls, over him, would fawn.

There once was a man from Belize
Who had a huge urge to sneeze.
His nose was itching
Because he was snitching
Forbidden fruit under the trees.

A man-hating stripper from Leicester
Had boils she encouraged to feicester.
They seemed to detract
From the strength of her act
But at least no-one tried to moleicester.

Once out on the lake at Dubuque
A girl took a row with a Duque
He remarked "I am sure
You are honest and pure"
Then leaned right over to puke

There was a young woman from Madrid
Who was longing to have a kid
Then came an Italian
With balls like a stallion
And rode her like Billy the Kid.

There was a man from Niagra Falls,
Who toured all the music halls,
His greatest trick
Was to stand on his prick,
And roll off the stage on his balls.

There once was a man name of Able,
Who played with himself 'neath the table,
His organ was lengthy,
And tremendously strengthly,
Our Able should live in a stable.

There once was a plumber named Lee
Who was plumbing his girl by the sea
She said "stop plumbing,
there's somebody comeing"
Said the plumber still plumbing "it's me!"

I'd rather have fingers than toes,
I'd rather have ears than a nose,
And a happy erection,

Brought just to perfection,
Makes me terribly sad when it goes!

There once was an alien from Venus,
who had a 20 inch penis.
When day turned to night,
he though it was alright,
and wiped it off with a kleenex.

J. Edgar, he knew that the crux
Of gangster control was big bucks.
Some said he was queer,
But that was a smear;
It's the other Hoover that sucks.

There was a young man from D.C.
Who went to the men's room to pee.
While acting the fool,
He pulled out his tool,
And pissed on himself and on me.

There was a young fella named Bubb,
Who played with himself in the tub.
Massaging his balls,
He shot on the walls
While farting out rub-ah-dub-dub.

Nymphomaniacal Jill
Tried a dynamite stick for a thrill
They found her vagina
Way over in China
And bits of her tits in Brazil

There once was a maiden from Chichester
whose beauty made saints in their niches stir.
One Sunday in mass
she dared show her ass, and
made the Bishop of Chichester's britches stir.

Here's to the girl named Louise
Who's pussy hair hung to her knees
The crabs got together
and Knitted a sweater
So in the winter her pussy wouldn't freeze.

There once was horndog named Schuller
Who measured his dick with a ruler
He found out his dong
Was an inch 'n' a half long
Then he turned off the lights so he'd fool her!

There once was a man named Doug
Who had an abroller on his rug
On it he was wacking
Goin to town just jacking
Trying to fill up his drinking mug

The couple, they jumped in the sack
With her legs wrapped tight 'round his back
But a condom, they found
Was nowhere around
So he couldn't slip into her crack.

There once was a lady from Madras,
Who didn't know what to do with 'er ass,
She wanted to Fart,
And tried with all heart,
And now it is just shit that she has.

There once was a girl named Hortence
Whose boobies were simply immence
One day while playing soccer
She confused the ball with her knocker
And kicked it right over the fence!

There was once a man from Bulgaria
who went for a piss in an area
said waiter to cook

Oh do come and look
Have you ever seen anything hairier?

The Postmaster General Cried 'Arsehole'
A pair of Bulls Balls in a parcel
Stamped IRA
with nine pence to pay
Addressed to the King, Windsor Castle

Spouse of a pretty young thing
came home from war in the spring
he was lame, but he came
with his hand on his cane
a discharge is a wonderful thing

there once was a man named steve
who always wanted to leave
he went next door
and found a whore
and now when i see him,i heave

There once was a girl from GA
who spent her days whoring away
when asked,"Goes it well"
she says,"Really can't tell,
that is till my customers pay.

There once was a man from Florida
That liked a man's wife so he borrowed her
When they got into bed
he said may God strike me dead
This isn't a vagina its a corridor.

There once was a farm boy named jake
who yearned so much for a date
when he ran out of luck
he made due with a duck
The village priest pronounced them husband and mate

There was once a boy from Milande
who thought caressing his penis was grand
but he looked in displeasure
at the white, sticky measure
of goo it left in his hand.

There once was a man with no shame
On his wife he would place all the blame
So behind peoples eyes
He would pull out his prize
Once was caught d$%^ in hand to explain!

There once was a lady from khartoum
whos untouched flower had reached it's full bloom
While waiting for a mate
she reached a feverish state
and ended up making due with a broom!

There once was a fireman named Rick
Who thought he was really quite slick
He would go all over town
Waving his hose all around
Thinking it would impress the chicks

A serial kisser named Tucker
Would approach every lass with a pucker.
But sometimes his mouth
Went a trifle far South
And landed where others might fuck 'er.

From the depths of the crypt of StGiles
came a scream that resounded for miles.
Said the vicar "Good gracious!
Has Father Ignatious
forgotten the Bishop has piles?"

The new cineramic emporium
Is not just a super-sensorium,
But a highly effectual

Heterosexual
Mutual masterbatorium.

There was an old scott named McTavish
who attempted an anthropoid ravish.
The object of rape
was the wrong sex of ape,
And the anthropoid ravished McTavish.

There was a young girl of Baroda
who built an erotic pagoda;
The walls of its halls
were festooned with the balls
And the tools of the fools that bestrode her.

I met a lewd nude in Bermuda,
Who thought she was shrewd ; I was shrewder;
She thought it was crude
To be wooed in the nude;
I pursued her,subdued her and screwed her.

There was ayoung man named Sam.
Who was quite proud of his ham.
One day while getting head.
His girlfriend looked up and said,
"This damn thing tastes like Spam".

There was a blonde cutey named Patty
Who found a rich sugar daddy
This businesslike quail
Made dough off her tail
Now she drives a convertible caddy.

There once was a girl from Nantukit
Whose only hobby is to suck it
She likes a big dick
One she can lick
She swallows, gets sick and upchucks it

A flatulent lady named Marta
was widely renowned as a Farter
On the strength of one bean
she'd fart "God Save The Queen"
And Beethoven's "Moonlight Sonata"

When the Bermondsey Bricklayers struck,
Bill Bloggins was havin' a f**k.
By Union rules
he had to lay down his tools.
Now wasn't that hard bleedin' luck!

There once was a priest from Dundee,
Who went in the alley to pee,
Dominiscus Nobiscum
Oh why don't the piss come,
It must be the C_L_A_P.

To his wife said the new wed Detective
Could it be that my eyesights defective
or has the East tit the least bit
the best of the West tit,
Or is it a faulty perspective?

A young girl from Ekatahuna
was laid in her bunk on a Schooner
This nautical ride
left her something inside
We'll know just what in nine months or sooner

There was a young lady from Crewe
Who said, as the Bishop withdrew
"The Vicar was quicker
and slicker and thicker
And nine inches longer than you"

There once was a man named booker
who only like to fuck hookers
one day at the loft

his dick fell off
and now he's only a looker.

There once was a guy called Reg
who fucked a girl in a hedge
then along came his wife
with a big carving knife
and cut off his meat and two veg.

There once was a girl from Seattle
Whose hobby was sucking off cattle
A bull from the south
Left a wad in her mouth
That made her ovaries rattle

There once was a man from Briton
Who said to his girl, you're a tight 'n
She cried 'pon my soul
You're in the wrong hole
There's plenty of room in the right one

there was once a guy called Alex Testa
Who looked alot like uncle festa
even his face
was a discrace
alex testa, blubber from manchester

There was a young housewife from Des Plaines,
Who was playing with the family"s Great Dane,
She said to her daughter,
"Bring a bucket of water,
I'm afraid that we're hung up again!"

A bearded old biker named Charlie
Took a very long ride on his Harley.
He knew that his hog
Created no smog,
'Cause he ran it on hops and malt barley.

There once was a girl from Maine
Who when fucked would experience pain
She said to her man
Listen up Dan
Get out of my rectal drain

There once was a girl called Crissy
Who had a very unusual pussy.
You could be eager to please
But it would just make you sneeze
Cuz it wasn't really a pussy, it was a cat.

There was an old Abbot most docile
Who found a remarkable fossil
He could tell from the bend
And the wart on the end
T'was the peter of Paul the Apostle.

There once was a whore named Jade
The most sought after trick in the trade
When she died she was laid
Then relaid in the shade
And no man will since part with his spade

There once was a girl on the net
When surfing she always got wet
She had miles and miles
of xxx files
Cyber sex was all she could get

there once was a silly old Widower
Who wanted to dance to the Fiddler
Though he had love in his heart
he fell for an old fart
who was the whole towns free Diddler

There once was a lady called Pam
Who took a trip on a tram
the fucking conductor

took out his constructor
and now shes wheeling a pram

there was a young professionel women from clyde,
whose surgeon cut open her hide,
he misplaced his stitches,
closed the wrong niches,
so now she does all her work on the side

There once was a lad from Nantucket
Who didn't need that damn bucket
He went to his wife
So sweet and so nice
Oh, please honey will you sucket

There once was a lad named Maurice(Morris)
Who went for a tryst with Doris
When asked how he fared
He answered with a stare
Damn! I was greatly victorious

There once lived a gravedigger named Jay
Who courted in an unusual way
The girls he would spoon
While staring up at the moon
Then he'd cover them back up with clay

There once was a gravedigger named Bert
Who was seduced by the wiles of a flirt
The two would lie prone
Until just before Dawn
Then she had to go back in the dirt

There was a young woman from winslow creek
who had her monthlies twice a week.
said a friend from woking
how provoking
no time for poking so to speak!

There was a boy who did not suck.
But he had the worst of luck.
He tripped in school,
and broke a rule,
It hurt so he said "fuck!"

There was a young lady named Brent
With a cunt of enormous extent
And so deep and so wide
The acoustics inside
Were so good you could hear when you spent.

While going down on my wife in our bed
The chandelier fell down on my head
If she didn't prefer this
That darn cunnelingis
It would have landed on my arse instead

A well hung young sailor named Bean
Could keep at it like a machine.
As he pummeled their ends,
His Society friends
All shouted out "God save the Queen!"

A lubricious young woman named Gwen
Had never learned how to say "when!"
So she did it again
And again and again
And again and again and again.

There was a lady from Kent
To a football game she went
she stood near the goal
and opened her hole
and in the football went!

There was once a boy named Hutch,
Men he liked to touch.
He did it with a rabbit,

It then became a habbit
And now he does it too much

A girl of the Enterprise crew
refused every offer to screw
Till a Vulcan named Spock
crawled under her smock
And now she is eating for two

The Enterprise girls so one hears
have chased Spock for several years
His look of disdane
has spared them great pain
For his prick is as sharp as his ears

The prick of the engineer Scott
fell off from Saturian Rot
So he went to the basement
and made a replacement
of tungsten and plastic and snot

A habit quite gross and unsavory
held the Bishop of Illi in slavery
With libidinous howls
he buggered young owls
that he kept in an underground avery

A Disturbing Tale Comes From Niger
Of A Lady, Her Donkey, And A Tiger
What Occurred In The Bush
Might Have Remained Hush Hush
But For The Ass Print On The Face Of The Tiger

There Was A Young Lady From Butte
Obsessed With A Man Of Repute
She Spent Many An Hour
Peeking In At His Shower
While Tuning The Strings Of Her Lute

There once was a man named O'Toole
Who kept his long tool on a spool
One cold night it unraveled
Into a convent it traveled
And was promptly chopped up as a Yule

"My Nieces are darling," said Sid.
"To oblige them I do as I'm bid."
As he tucked them in bed,
he asked: "What's to be read?"
"Uncle Rhemus," they cried, and he did.

There once was a fart deep within,
who thought that to stay was a sin,
So he tunneled about,
till he found his way out,
as I silently sat with a grin.

there was a young guy from Peru,
who dreamt he was eating his poo.
when he woke up
he had to upchuck
and then he was eating that too!

There was a young man from Zaire
Who tried to have sex with a bear
when the mean, nasty brute
took a swipe at his root
and left nothing but testes and hair!

There once was a man name of Ewing
Who thought,"why be bothered with screwing?
When its cheaper and cleaner
To finger your weiner
And besides, you can see what you're doing!"

There Once Was A Vicar Name Ben
Whose Body Was Exceedingly Thin
As He Whipped Out His Wicker

His Young Bride did Snicker
Until He Thrust In Up To His Chin

Very sex mad was Mr. Blubber
He loved to suck , fuck and bugger
But the joy of his life
Were the tits of his wife
One real and one Indian rubber

On Halloween a young girl from the Coast
Was screwed in the Park by a Ghost
At the height of Orgasm
This pale ectoplasm
Cried "I think I can feel it, almost"

There was a Stage Manager named Sherry
Who could handle all she could carry
She did "Twelve Angry Men"
Again and again
And left them all feeling quite merry.

There was an old farmer named Young
Who was quite remarkably hung.
When cleaning the stable,
his member was able
To serve as a fork for the dung.

The man in the bar was real shrewd
some may say a bit lewd
he reached out his mitts
looking for tits
but discovered the chest of a dude.

There Once Was A Gal From Vancouver
Who'd Suck On A Schlong Like A Hoover
Her Squeal Of Delight
Should Fill You With Fright
For God Alone Could Remoover

There once was a fireman named Gary,
Whose hose was nice and big, OH VERY!
His wife, she would pray
That his hose he would spray,
'Cuz that would make her merry.

Dykes or pliers said Kim,
can bend or cut wire of tin.
But when asked of which gender,
she'd prefer to "bend" her.
"Has two cuts and does not rhyme with tin"

Their once was a man named Joe
Who was an idiot,you know
He could not find
any change but a dime
So he then bought a cheap ho

There was a young man from Brazil
Who swallowed an Atom Bomb pill.
His bum back fired
His belly retired
And his willy shot over the hill

There was a young Scot named McAmiter
Who boasted excessive diameter
But it wasn't the size
That opened their eyes
Twas his rythmn, iambic pentameter

There was a young lady named Hilda
Who went on a date with a Builder
She knew that he could
And he should and he would
And he did, and it bloody nigh killed her!

There Once Was A Fellow Named Ken
Who Kept All Of His Pigs In A Pen
But A Lady From York

Ran Away With His Pork
And She Did It Again And Again

There once was a boy named nookie
Who sat on his girl friends cookie
She screamed real loud
And it made a big crowd
Then she said he won't get no more nookie

There once was a woman from Rhodesia
She would do anything to please ya
she said "it would be fine
if you fucked me from behind
I just hope my tapeworm doesn't sees ya."

There once was a man from Duluth
whose dick got shot off in his youth
He fucked with his nose
his fingers and toes
and came through a hole in his tooth

There once was a chick on the net
who decided to take a double dare bet
When she lifted her blouse
and clicked on her mouse
and found it was all soaking wet

The man from Brazil was so weird.
His friends said, 'It's perfectly clear.
He has a big dong
that he cleans all day long
by rubbing it on his long beard!'

The old drunk's dick was so wizened.
he said,'Oh my, I've been poisoned!
I had a long dong,
but now it's all gone.'
The cops said, 'Away it was pissened.'

There once was a young man named Fred,
who said "I must have some head."
The whores in Las Vegas
all said "But he ate us!"
So poor Fred then NEVER got head.

There once was a nasty old ho
Who opened up a bakery sto
You might not find it funny
But she saved lots of money
Because she had her own yeast for the dough

There was a young fellow from Yale
Whose face was exceedingly pale.
He spent his vacation
In self-masturbation
Because of the high price of tail.

A widow whose singular vice
was to keep her late husband on ice.
Said "It's been hard since I lost him-
Ill never defrost him!
Cold comfort, but cheap at the price.

There was a young fellow named Veach
Who fell fast asleep on the beach.
His dreams of nude women
Had his proud organ brimming
and Squirting on all within reach.

There was a young man from Vancouver
Whose existence had lost its prime mover,
But its loss he supplied
with a peice of bull's hide
Two pears, and the bag from the Hoover.

I know of a birthmark, wrote the scholar
That is shaped much like a silver dollar
It is on the spindle

Of my brother Windell
And he will gladly extend you a dollar

Thomas Turkey was a handsome lugger
His wife was sure fond of his sugar
But on a Thanksgiving Morn
He was stuffed full of corn
By the cook, who was a bit of a Bugger

I once stopped a Turkey named Gobble
To ask why he walked with a wobble
The cook has been pressing
My arse full of Dressing
And it's give me a bit of a nobble

As a child I had a puppy named Spot
Who swam daily in our chamber pot
I must truly admit
He stank like (crap)
But I loved that puppy a lot

There once was a fellow named Jeter
Who had a skeeter alight on his peter
He said 'Goody Goody'
I see some free-boody
And he probed it one-sixth of a meter

There once was a man named Spicolli
Who like to jack with his Ravioli
Loved boy's salad to toss
And drink their sauce
While holding his beefy stombolii

That is no comet you see hurling past Mars
But the jubilant wife of the giant man Lars
She applied proper torque
Until he popped his cork
Then she launched into orbit among the stars

The Worlds'largest Gal and it's smallest man
Their Courtship was doomed from the day it began
The night they wed
He took her to bed
and nine months later he was born again

There was a young man from Rabaul
Who had a rectangular ball
The square of his date
plus his penis times eight
Was two-fifths of five-eights of fuck all.

Tarzan swing through the air
Natives see his arse is bare
Tarzan go home to good wife Jane
His noble face fill with pain
How say he lose her underwear?

There was a young girl from Coleshill
Who sat one day on a moleshill
The resident mole
stuck his nose up her hole
Now Miss Coleshill alright but the mole's ill

There was a young man who had the art
Of making a capital tart.
With a handful of shit,
Some snot and a spit
And he flavors the whole with a fart.

There was a young lady from Phoenix,
Who stuffed her brassiere with some Kleenex.
She paid it no mind,
Since her boyfriend, in kind,
Used Scott Towels to augment his penix!

There lived a saintly girl from Sleepy Hollow
Who entertained the numerous men of the Wallow
When asked by Ichabod Crane:

"Have you a place I might drain?"
"No Thanks," she replied "I don't Swallow."

There once was a man from Wisconsin
Who had a three foot long johnson
While milking his cow
He fell on his plow
And now sex is no fun

The passengers all were delighted,
The stewardesses too were excited,
Up there in the void,
They really enjoyed
The pleasure of flying United!

A hapless young laddie from Poole
Had a nut on the end of his tool
When he went to unscrew it
His Pa said "dont do it,
or your arse will fall off, you young fool"!

An old mathmetician named Hall
Wrote a theorom not hard to recall
To prove it was wrong
That the length of his Schlong
Was four fifths of five eighths of Fuck All

There once was a man named Brewster,
Who said to his wife as he goosed her,
That used to be grand,
But just look at my hand,
Your not wiping as good as you used to!

The general commanding Fort Totten
Had a habit both snobbish and rotten:
He made men of high ranks
Open left and right flanks
While their privates were mostly forgotten.

There once was a girl who said, "No"
and all the boys called her a "Ho"
and when she was asked why
she simply replied
I have a warm dildo at home.

A young lady from Ashton Le Stairs
Had five large breasts and seven small spares
there were four in a line
the effect was divine
whilst the others were formed up in squares

A young fellow from Brighton Le Sands
has sores on the palms of his hands
which look like a blister
and so does his sister
And they're both blind, or so one understands

There was a young man from Atlantis
Who took off an Amazon's panties
And took her to bed
Where she cut off his head
But he carried on, just like a Mantis

Blow said the wind........Blow like me
Pucker your lips...It's easy as can be
I will try said the girl
....But why in the world
Did you address me as....Miss Lewinski

There once was an intern from Vermouth
Who was fired when she broke a tooth
Dictating a Bill
On Capital Hill
She could not pronounce Arkansooth

There was once a sailor from whales,
An Expert at pissing in gales,
He could piss in a jar

from the top-gallent spar.
Without even wetting the sails.

There was an old lady from Wheeling.
Who had a peculiar feeling.
She laid on her back
And opened her crack
And pissed all over the ceiling

There was an old lady of Ypres
Who got shot in the ass by some snipers,
And when she blew air
Through the holes that were there,
She astonished the cameron pipers.

I sat by the Dutches at tea
and she asked, "Do you fart when you pee?"
I said with some wit,
"Don you belch when you shit?
And felt it was one up for me.

There was an old scholar named Nick
who wrote latin and greek with his prick.
He peed a pecan
in the snow by a john
in a script more than three inches thick

There was a young lady of Newcastle
who wrapped up a turd in a parcel,
And sent it to a relation.
with this invitation-
"It has just come out from my arsehole"

There was a young woman from Wild
Who kept herself quite undefiled
By thinking of Jesus,
Contagious diseases,
And the bother of having a child.

As Titian was mixing rose madder
He spied a young nude on a ladder.
Her position, to Titian,
Suggested coition,
So he climbed up the ladder and had 'er.

There was a young novice of Chichester
Whose form made the saints in their niches stir.
One morning at matins
Her bosom 'neath satins
Made the bishop of Chichester's britches stir.

There once was a guy named Dane,
Who liked to sing in the rain.
He made fun of an old man,
Who's name was Dan,
But then he got beat with a cane!

There once was a man named Keith
Who circumcised men with his teeth
He didn't do it for leisure
Or sexual pleasure
But did it for the cheese underneath

A sultan who likes his girls buxom
At ninety still often abducts 'em
And then they are led
To a sumptuous bed
In which he regretfully tucks 'em.

On Kristen's great Website please click,
Though some naughty limericks are sick,
Which you might disdain,
There's some sweet and plain,
And others that cut to the quick.

There once was a man from South Ealing
Who found his prick highly appealing
But not to feel dumb

He made his hand numb
So it was like someone else he was feeling

I knew an old geezer named Caesar
He tried O his darndest to please her
Though overly stout
And well-known as a lout
He managed to tickle and tease her !

I once knew a dame from Poughkeepsie
Who tucked away bootlegg-ed whiskey
She stuffed all her hockings
Beneath her blue stockings
One nip of her tuck made him tipsy !

There once was a virgin at Penn State
Whose hunger just would not abate.
He said with a grin,
What a sin it'd have been
If I ate out my date on a plate.

There once was a woman named Patti ,
Who was concerned about being a fatty,
She met a man named Garry,
Who was really quite scary,
And he bopped the fatty, off Patti !!

There once was a man from New York
Whose penis was shaped like a fork.
While screwing his wife,
Who was shaped like a knife
They could carve up a really nice pork!

A young lady was fond of a stunt
so she took of her clothes in a punt
she uncorked some Champaign
and without any shame
she sprayed it all over her front

A young lady with dubious style
liked to take off her clothes for a while
she'd get down on her knees
and mainly to please
she'd show off her verticle smile

A girl with magnificent tits
when dancing would wiggle her hips
a wonderful flirt
she'd lift up her skirt
and exhibit her sensuous lips

there was a young man named boc
who had a seventy inch cock
he fell off a chair
poll vaulted through the air
now he can wank with a sock!!

there was a young man who sent e-mails,
to various dubious females,
when axked what they said,
he just shook his head,
i'd rather not go into details.

To the penis of old Mr. Schuster
Was attached an electrical booster
In a screw with Miss Drew
his main rheostadt blew
and it felt like a snowblower had goosed her!

There once was a guy named Dave
Who wanted a good close shave.
His razor did stick,
He cut off his dick
And now he's a eunich slave!

There was a man called Motar
who often rode on a scooter
His favorite trick

was to stand on his prick
and use his arse as a hooter

A Lady asked me to tea
and said "do you fart when you pee?"
I said with some whit
"do you belch when you shit?"
I think that was one up to me

There was a young girl from Utoxeter
so pretty that men waved their cocks at her
one went so far
as to wave from his car
a cock all riddled with pox at her

There once was a troubadour named Gibbon
who did sing for a livin'
I onced asked him why
this was his reply
"I just do it to meet horny women."

There once was a slut named Bobby
Who was blowing a boy named Robie
When I told her to stop
His penis she droped
"But this is my favorite hobby!"

A certain young lady named Allus
Lunched with the king at the Pallus
The dirty old twat
Said look what ive got
And promptly showed her his phallus

There once was a man from Iran,
Who fried his nuts in a pan,
He said with a shout,
"PUT THE FIRE OUT!"
And he went running to his girlfriend Ann.

There was a young girl from Australia,
who painted her cunt like a Dahlia.
At 5 pence a smell,
it was all very well,
but 10 pence a lick was a failure.

There once was a girl called Kim,
who had an allmighty quim.
It wasn't the size
that attracted the flies,
but the crystalized cum round the rim.

There was a young lady named Beti
Who was having sex with a Yeti
When they started to cum
The resulting hum
Upset the scanners at Seti

A dominant lady named Yael
Liked to beat on her slaves with a flail
Sayin' "Be lookin cute,
While you're lickin' my boot,
And continue on up to my tail!"

One evening with forethought and malice
A horny gal travelled to Dallas
She liked to play cowboy
Saying, "hey, you be my boy
Just bring on the whips and your phallus!"

Though she knew it had grown to a fetus.
She felt rumblings come not from her uterous,
So the pregnancy thought,
Was a pregnancy not.
It was really her stomach quite tumorous.

I knew a Jess looking for laboar.
So I said she should be a proffessore.
But the Mrs. Resources

Said "Whoa! Hold your horses"
We don't hire no dopped up old crack whores.

I once knew a Christiane Why,
Who though tried couldn't satisfy guys.
Then a Calvin she met
Who said "Girl, don't you fret.
You won't gag my inadequate size."

There was once a beautiful palace,
'Side the sea, with a vine covered trellis.
And where?.. ..Up beyond,
Yonder oaks, leafy frond,
Rose a turret, tall, shaped of mine phallus.

A girl I once knew named Melania,
Used to lick her own boobs with her tongue, yeah!
But she'd suck them too hard,
For one day, on her yard,
They sprayed milk out, don't get any on ya!

there was a young caveman named Ug
who stuck his plug in a jug.
said ug with a shrug
as he gave it a tug,
'Now ain't this a hell of a fug'

I wooed a stewed nude in Bermuda,
I was lewd, but my God! she was lewder.
She said it was crude
To be wooed in the nude-
I pusued her, subdued her, and screwed her!

There once was a man from Goshem
Who took out his balls to Wash'em
His wife said JACK
If you don't put em BACK
I'll stand on the buggers and squash em

There was an old man on a bench
Who created a terrible stench
He had hairs up his nose
Where grass sometimes grows
And his wife was a stupid old wench

Charlotte the harlot from hell
said, "I wish my body would sell,
But it seems that no buyer,
Is filled with desire,
By the peculiar way that I smell"

"I have serviced this town for years,
Since the days that gays were just queers
I provided most of the gentry,
With their first entry,
And now all I hear are their jeers".

Bill, an Arkansian president,
While in the White House resident,
Did his staff of office display,
In a most unusual way,
Then claimed it was JFK's precedent.

There was a young girl of Surrey
Who only ate spicy curry
She tried a pie and
Stuck it up her nigh
That weird young lady of Surrey

There once was a girl from New York
whose vagina was plugged with a cork.
To remove it she fingered,
but still the cork lingered.
So she got it out with a fork.

There once was a girl from Manila,
who had a face that looked like Godzilla.
She could screw you real fine,

while swinging from a vine,
and give you head just like a gorilla.

There once was a girl from Tucker
Who wanted a canary to pluck her
She tightly squeezed her "Vaginer"
But it flew up her "Hiner"
And was killed by a runaway trucker

There was a young man from Stroud,
Who was feeling his date in a crowd,
When a man up in front,
went," Sniff, sniff, Cunt!"
Just like that, not loud.

There was a young man from Peru
who lived off pox droppings and spew
when he couldn't get this
he ate shit and drank piss
and he looked fucking well on it too

there was a young girl from East Cheam
who crept into the vestry unseen
she took down her knickers
and likewise the vicar's
and said "how about it old bean".

There once was a boy named ali
He took all the girls with glee
But when they unzipped his fly
he wanted to die
cuz his wee was the size of a flea

There once was a girl named Robyn
every night her bed was a bobbin'
the men would take leave
after being quite pleased
and leave Robyn with her body a throbbin'

long ago once in ancient Japan
was a geisha who dressed as a man
her pants were so tight
that they rubbed her just right
when she walked you might say that she ran

A masturbating gourmand from Hanoi
With a tool that resembled Bok Choi
What came in his hand
Looked like Moo Goo Gai Pan
So he garnished it with duck sauce and soy

The bishop one Sunday, in the lurch
After eating a pound of spoiled perch
Emitted a blast
In the middle of mass
That extinguished all the candles in church

A strapping fellow from Australia
After his fortnightly bacchanalia
Buggered a dog
Three mice and a frog
And a bishop in fullest regalia

My tool, it was a throbbin'
and I needed a knobbin'
but being at work
I weren't free to jerk
so I dreamed of Carole's head bobbin'

There once was a young idler named Blood
Made a fortune performing at stud
With a fifteen-inch peter
A double-beat metre
And a load like the Biblical Flood

I think the feeling is grand
Of holding my gland in my hand
But what I really want to do

Is become Johnny Apple-goo
And spread my seed all over the land

There once was a man from Manila
who lived with 5 girls in a villa.
When they'd go to bed
they loved giving head
cause he'd soak it all day in vanilla.

The tale of the chef from France
A victim of drunk circumstance
Though he burned the baguette
What he lived to regret
Was the loaf that he pinched in his pants

The inventor from India said
"I made a turbin from butter instead!"
To the Punjab's surprise
When his pancakes arrived
They served them on top of his head

'Tis a legend in all of Madras
The lass with the breasts of glass
In a sad twist of fate
She fought with her mate
And they smashed when she fell on her ass

Of the indian man Sanjay
Who ate too much curry one day
Though he crapped in Bopahl
It is said by them all
That it stunk all the way to Bombay!

The legend of Indian Chief Eno
Said "thank God they don't know what we know...
Don't fight the white man
Just give 'em the land
Fuck 'em, we'll start a casino!!"

The overweight lady named Tammy
Fell in the ochestra pit in Miami
All of the brass
Went straight up her ass
She farted, and she won a Grammy!!

An alien cam down here from Venus.
Not a girl, but a guy (had a penis).
With three eyes in between,
Pointed ears that were green.
He was obviously not of our Genus.

He landed at old Johnson's farm.
An arrival that caused some alarm
To old Johnson's daughter.
Who thought if he caught her.
He might want to cause her some harm

Now our alien wasn't too bright.
He forgot to bring something to light
The night and his way
Through the field filled with hay
Took a left instead of a right.

Now things didn't turn out like they aughter
He did not meet up with the daughter
Instead he found Bessie
And now things get messy.
He not only found her but caught her.

"My Dear you have beautiful eyes!"
"Big and brown like Venutian Creme Pies"
"I can't wait to show mother
Your soft silky utter."
(You're going to be such a surprise.)

From behind the clouds came the moon,
As the alien continued to spoon.
And old Johnson's girl

Let the curtains unfurl
To a scene that made her heart swoon.

See the alien was wearing no frock
And Ms. Johnson was given a shock
She believed not her eyes
For there 'tween his thighs
Was an 18 inch glowing green cock.

And so to the steps she alighted.
There were things she just knew must be righted
Tell this guy with the cow
Just exactly how
With her he'd be truly delighted.

She ran through the field up to him.
Stuck her hand out and said "My name's Kim"
And you sir are hot
Look here what I got
For you. It's a seldom used quim.

"I'm sorry deary but right now.
I am currently courting this cow."
The alien said
Then Kim nearly dropped dead
(Oh my god he just licked his eye brow)

Now Kim was determined as ever
To succeed in this lustful endeavor
And spend the whole night
In the blissful delight.
She was sure the alien would deliver.

She was sure he'd see Bess was a dud.
Just standing there chewing her cud.
It soon became plain
His lust she'd not gain.
Cause he started in pounding his pud.

But it was the last thing that she saw
That for Kim was the camel's last straw
The alien's tongue
Licked Bess's bung
And a smile split the alien's maw.

Oh Bessie my dear let's make haste
To Venus there's no time to waste
That taste oh..oh my!
Venutian creme pie!
And to the space ship the two raced.

Into the welkin they shot
Leaving poor Kim really hot
For and 18 inch dick
And a tongue oh so quick
So she laid down and played with her twat.

There once was a girl named Spears
Who wanted to enlarge her brassieres
she went to get it
and yup you bet it
now its timblerlake and Spears

There once was a man from Lancaster
who, while eating, befell a disaster
his bowels, well loaded
swelled up and exploded
and filled his nice knickers with plaster

There once was a girl from Kentucky
who considered herself quite lucky.
She'd unzip the fly
of just any old guy
and never found one that was yucky

I'm Darwin, I had an erection
Of several square inches cross-section
So I set out to screw

Every Duchess I knew
In the interest of natural selection

The Queen and the Duke were dismayed,
to find Andy and Koo had once played.
As for Charlie and Ed,
well, enough has been said
'bout the damsels that they might have layed.

There was a young actress from Crewe,
Who remarked as the vicar withdrew,
The Bishop was quicker,
 and thicker and slicker,
And two inches longer than you.

There was a young vampire called mable,
whose periods were always quite stable,
at every full moon

she took out a spoon,
and drank herself under the table.

There was a young plumber from Lee,
who was plumbing his girl with great glee,
she said stop your plumbing,
I think someone's coming,
said the plumber still plumbing "its me"!

A kinky young girl from Bexhill,
Tried a dynamite stick for a thrill,
They found her vagina,
 in North Carolina,
and bits of her tits in Brazil.

There was a young man from Pitlocherie,
making love to his girl in the rockery,
she said look you've cum,
all over my bum,
This isn't a shag it's a mockery.

There was a young lassie from Morton,
who had one long tit and one short 'en,
on top of all that, a great hairy twat,
and a fart like a six fifty Norton.

There was a young girl called Molly,
who fancied a bit in a quarry.
She laid on her back, and opened her crack.
And the bastard backed in with a lorry.

There was a young man from Harrow,
who had one as big as a marrow.
He said to his tart, try this for a start.
My balls are outside on a barrow.

There was a young girl from Hitchen,
who was scratching her crutch in the kitchen.
Her mother said "Rose,
its crabs I suppose".
She said "bollocks, get on with your knitting"

There once was a man named Kent
Whose d*ck was so long it was bent
To stay out of trouble
He'd stick it in double
Instead of cumming he went!

A Rabbi who lived in Peru
Was vainly attempting to screw
His wike said " Oy Vey "
If you keep on this way
The Messiah will come before you do!

There once was man named Springer
Whose testicles got caught in the wringer
He hollered in pain
As they rolled down the drain
(in a high voice) There goes my career as a singer!

There once was a man named Bruno
Who said "Screwing is one thing I do know
Oh, women are fine
And sheep are devine
But Llamas are numero uno!"

There once was a man from Dealing
Who pounded his pud with great feeling
Then like a trout
He'd stick his mouth out
And wait for the drops from the ceiling.

There once was a man from Sprocket
Whose dick got caught in a socket
His wife, the old bitch
She flipped on the switch
And his ass lit up like a rocket!

Beneath the spreading Chestnut tree
The village idiot sat
Amusing himself
By abusing himself
And catching the drops in his hat!

There once was a millwright named Mac
Who loved to look at men's crack
So he went for a scrub
With his hand on his chub
And said "boy, I wish I had one like that!"

There was a young man clad in plastic.
His sexuall styles were quite drastic!
Handcuffed to the bed
He'd f*** 'till he bled
Then beg to be whipped with elastic!

There once was a boy who liked yeast
And bread was only the least
He got him a ho

She had sour dough
So he spread 'em and had him a feast!

The young lady tickled my chin
And said, "Would you like to get in?"
I said "Oh you bet"
Then broke in a sweat
And worried like hell about sin!

Outside the hard rain was a-fallin"
In my bed we laid about ballin'
When the lightnin', she struck,
It sure ruined our fuck
And set up a great caterwaulin'!

I once knew a girl named Pleasant
Who was from the town of Mount Pleasant
Receptive was she
To my earnest plea
What a joy it was to mount Pleasant!

There was a man from Cape Tongas
Whose balls were really humongous
He required a sling and a hoist
And a wheelbarrow, of course
In order to walk among us!

A lovely young starlet named Smart
Was asked to display oral art,
As the price for a role.
She complied, met this goal,
And then sank her teeth in the part.

There once was a man from Iraq
Who had holes down the length of his cock.
When he got an erection
He could play a selection
By Johann Sebastian Bach.

A bearded old biker named Charlie
Took a very long ride on his Harley
He knew that his hog
Created no smog
'Cause he ran it on hops and malt barley!

He rode through old West Virginia
Which is very far from Gdynia
He picked up a girl
Whom he took for a whirl
And when done said,"I'd like to get in ya."

There was an old lecher named Boone
Who took his Viagra too soon.
The hooker was late
And he was left to his fate.
He was found on the floor in a swoon.

Now, the loveliest ladies in Visalia
Are best known for snug fit genitalia.
When you enter their space,
You well know it's a race
To see who first makes point interalia.

There once was a young man from Dallas
Who so frequently fondled his phallus
That the organ turned red
Then it blistered and bled
And developed a very large callus.

Once was a man named La Fong
Who had a most bodacious schlong
High testosterone
Caused a permanent bone
And the ladies won't leave him alone.

Miss Lewinsky and Clinton went far
With their sexual acts most bizarre,
But the substitute phallus

I thought was quite callous
As you can't light a soggy cigar!

Dear Monica, I have to confess
We have made such a terrible mess
How would we know
When you gave me a blow
That it would end up all over your dress?

If Shakespeare were writing today
About Toastpoint, I know he would say,
Include my Limericks,
With the assorted pricks,
That came here to lyrically play.

A boatman by the name of DeFarge
Had a pecker exceedingly large.
He was arrested one day,
For public foreplay,
With two pleasure craft & a barge.

Miss Lewinsky, Miss Tripp and Ken Starr
Were out for a night in a bar
With Trippy onlooking
Ken and Mon started cooking,
Smartly spewing into a jar!

Montezuma's revenge isn't sweet
And on the bus, it isn't so neat
Riding tween towns
With my head hanging down
The shit spewed all over my feet!

There was once a brave knight of Camelot
Who liked to use his hands a lot.
He was often seen,
With Guinevere the queen,
And no one was quite sure about Sir Lancelot.

There was an old ape in the zoo
He had a humongous wazoo
When erect, it was scary
All scabrous and hairy
It frightened the elephants, too!

Once an old geezer from Boston
Went for a ride in an Austin
Just room for his ass
A small can of gas
His balls wouldn't fit so he tossed 'em.

There once was a lady named McBagg
And to all the ladies she did brag
"My breasts are sizeable
And easily recognizeable
I never have to wear a name tag."

There is a lady who you'll
See sucking the tool of a mule
When the mule does bray
She had best get away
Or she'll gag on a pool of its spew'll!

There once was a White House intern who said,
"I've been in the Chief Executive's bed,
And three times a day
Bill Clinton would say,
'Come here, baby, give me head.'"

There was an old man in Brazil
Who swallowed a little blue pill
It gave him a charge
Made his penis grow large
And he gave all the ladies a thrill!

A curious mammal's the beaver
But the one's women carry are teasers
Men lose their shirts

When girls lift their skirts
And then chop off their pricks with a cleaver!

"Hey, waiter, my soup's got a fly in!"
He's swimmin, or it looks like he's tryin
And speakin of flies,
I may unzip mine
Cause my snake with me wants to dine.

The exiled Queen of Bulgaria
Had a crotch that grew hairier and hairier
When a young man named Tucker
Decided to fuck her
He had to hunt for her cunt with a terrier.

There was a young man from Bombay
Who was laying his girl on a sleigh
The weather was cold
His balls, they froze
So all he could shoot was frappe'.

There was a young man from Adair
Who was laying his wife on a stair
The bannister broke
He doubled his stroke
And polished her off in mid-air!

As Titian was preparing the matter
His model climbed up a ladder
Her position to Titian
Suggested coition
So he climbed up the ladder and had her!

There was a young man from Racine
Who invented a screwing machine
Concave or convex
It could screw either sex
And jerk itself off in between.

Let us now broach a ferkin to Durkin
Addicted to jerkin' his gherkin
His wife said, "Now Durkin
By jerkin' yer gherkin
Yer shirkin' yer firkin, you Bastard!!!

"The Impeachment" has moved to the Senate -
And Clinton still thinks he can win it -
But Trent Lott wants to see
Inside Monica's "V"
To check if Bill's cock is still in it.

There once was a bloke from Van Geeling,
Who would pound his pud with great feeling!
Then, like a trout,
He would stick his mouth out,
And wait for the drops from the ceiling!

Now that poor pothead from Australia,
His dong's much shorter, I tell ya!
He's sworn off coke,
Since damaging his poke,
Claiming total genital failure!

Why Monica, love your blue dress!
But my dear what is this white mess?
I know you and Billy
Got silly with his willy
But why can't you two confess?

A philosopher, finding a stone
Bent over to look with a groan.
This caught the eye
Of a bull passing by
Who drove him straight to his home!

If Shakespeare were writing today
He would write in a much different way.
No concern for the phonics

He would write in ebonics
"What Up! Poor Yoric!" he'd say.

Mathematics: of sciences, queen -
Exactly what does that mean?
Are math guys all gay
Or in some other way
Of sciences: number two, on the scene.

Miss Lewinsky, Miss Tripp and Ken Starr
All in search of the elusive cigar
One would just feel it
The other would steal it
While Ken sniffs the evidence jar.

Montezuma's revenge isn't sweet
For the things that it does to your seat
Makes your fundament sore
Like your ass has been bored
By a dick made of solid concrete!

Said Delilah to Samson, "Your hair
Turned me on when it used to be there...
Now to realize my fears
A dick with two ears
Takes its place on your shoulders so fair!

The whole trouble with airlines is planes
That's why everyone always complains
Cause carry-on's blow
And you know they should go
Up the passengers asses sideways.

One fine morning Mahatma Gandhi
Had a hard-on, and it was a dandy.
So he said to his aide,
"Quick, bring me a maid,
Or a goat, or whatever is handy!"

There once was a girl named Louise
Whose cunt hair grew down to her knees
The crabs in her twat
Tied the hair in a knot
And constructed a flying trapeze.

Starr's attackers are forming a mob.
They all hate him for doing his job.
In spite of Bill's mess
On Monica's dress
We are told we should CREDIT the slob!

Judge Thomas was said to have lied,
And Packwood was chased till he flied.
Condemnation so hearty
All depends on your party,
Since Willie still gets a free ride.

There was an old man from Orleans
Who sprouted a bulge in his jeans.
He'd walked in the park
'Till long after dark
But couldn't locate the latrines.

An alternate universe thrives
In which I may lead other lives.
My beck is my call!
Now pour a high-ball!
(They're *much* cheaper than hyper-drives.)

The mate went to drink a night-cap.
He fished out cap's crank with a grap.
He had to suck hard.
The piss-pipe was scarred,
'Cause cappy had died of the clap.

Don't know what is so fucking cool,
Unless it's the tip of my tool.
It seems there's a draft

From yo momma's aft.
Her fart-blasts are drying her drool.

She told me I was pretty sweet,
Yet misses your miniscule meat.
No wonder. Her bung
Now leaks spunky dung -
The kind that she tells me you eat.

A crippled old captain named Jed
Once kept a dead ram near his bed.
His crew thought him queer
When stuffed up its rear,
But Jed was just using the head.

There once was a girl named Louise,
Whose cunt hair hung to her knees.
The crabs in her twat
Tied it into a knot
And made thamselves a flying trapeze!

Why Monica, love your blue dress!
The Prez upon it has made a mess!
His aim should have been better,
While dictating that letter,
Else he wouldn't've had to confess!

There once was a girl from Hoboken
Who claimed that her cherry'd been broken,
By riding a bike
Down a cobblestone pike,
But it had really been broken from pokin'!

A privileged client's attorney
Who predictably called himself Bernie
Said "Lapsis linguae
gives all things away
so you might just end up on a gurney!"

"Hey, waiter, my soup's got a fly in!"
Whadda a stupid fuckin' place for him to die in
This ain't no damn joke
He's doin' the breast stroke
Cause the soup's so hot that he's fryin'!

Said a dentist, "Ma'am, please open wider
Cause here comes the skin-covered glider
The pink steel drill
The unpickled dill
A gift from your service provider!"

While swimming across the Zambezi
I encountered something thick and quite greasy
A translucent glob
An island of gob
Of the goo that comes out when ya squeeze me!

An anonymous poet online
In a really short period of time
Can compose something lewd
Usually quite crude
Except all those limericks of mine!

An eagle whose wings had been clipped
"I'm short", he quite dryly quipped
"not only my wings
But afew other things
Like my beak and my balls and my dick!"

There once was a young man from Rangoon
Who was born nine months too soon.
He didn't have the luck
To be born by a fuck,
He was scraped off the sheets with a spoon!

There once was a young girl named Anheiser
Who said that no man could surprise her.
Pabst took a chance

And found a Schlitz in her pants,
And now she's sadder Budweiser!

There once was a Bishop from Puno
Who said "There is one thing I do know
Little girls are all right
Little boys are too tight
But the Llama is Numero Uno!"

A nubile young Nubian nun
Would lift her black habit in fun;
But though she was bare
Underneath, none knew where
Habit ended, and nun had begun.

Regarding that Nubian nun,
Who played peekaboo on the run;
I'd say rather smartly
She acted most tartly.
(Forgive me for stooping to pun.)

That part of the bod is unsung,
But the thought of it keeps me quite young.
The name I can't tell,
But it does have a smell,
And it's right on the tip of my tongue.

The legs, as the body's main prop,
Are essential to stand, walk, or hop;
And they've been so designed
That when seen from behind,
The bottom, you'll find, is on top.

There was an old bullfrog from Prague
Who sat by the road on a log.
"Come and kiss me," he cried
To a princess he spied;
So she did and turned into a frog.

"Can you increase the size of my clit?"
Said Anita, somewhat of a twit.
"See, my husband's so small,
I can't feel him at all,
And the S.O.B. can't fuck for shit!"

Said Dr. Blum, a West Virginian
While he examined Dan O'Binion,
"You may well get the fidgets
When I insert two digits,
But YOU asked for a second opinion.

Behold a remarkable sight:
And IRS guy who's polite;
If fact he's quite gay,
One thinks that he may
Create a new kind of "tax bite"!

When Cain in a fit of vexation,
Slew Abel, divine condemnation
Was swift and gave pain;
If he tried it now, Cain
Would likely get three years probation.

A lady named Eve wasn't heedin'
Or didn't know much about readin'.
She ignored a clear sign
That said, "Here Do Not Dine",
And got her ass thrown out of Eden.

Back in Eden on that fateful day
God: "Where's Eve?" To which Adam did say:
"Sex surpasses my dream,
Now Eve's down in the stream."
God: "Damn. The fish will all smell that way."

An eloquent young man named Demude
Said, "The family allowance is crude;

Every time a Quebecker
Whips out his old pecker,
Some taxpayer in Ontario gets screwed.

He expected his lust would be realized
When he hit on the lady who tantalized.
He said, "Hey, pretty legs!
How do you like your eggs
In the morning?" She answered: "Unfertilized!"

They have simplified law for the gentry
Who want everything elementary.
Now rape's an offense
That makes much better sense:
It's a subclass of illegal entry.

An old archaeologist Throstle
Discovered a marvellous fossil.
He knew from the ratchet
And the knob that would catch it,
'Twas the pawl of Peter the Apostle.

A virgin of the female gender
Died because the doc couldn't mend her.
Her epitaph
Engendered a laugh;
"Returned unopened to sender."

A guy who would not run with women
Said, "Women should walk or go swimmin'.
You know it's a fact--
They tend to distract
With their bouncin' and shakin' and shimmin'."

A wild bucolic sex kitten,
Whose beau, with her charms, was so smitten,
He suggested some head,
She smiled shyly and said,
"Are we talking 'bout givin' or gittin'?"

On meeting each girl, he thought, "Could he?"
Disregarding the question of "Should he?"
His pants would reveal
His permanent zeal,
So that's why they all called him "Woody."

A globe-trotting man from St. Paul
Made a trip to Japan in the fall.
One thing he found out,
As he rambled about,
Was that Japanese ladies St. Taul.

A sentry on guard in a thicket,
Met a milk-maid exposing her wicket.
In exchange for some coins,
He united their loins,
And soon after became a pocked picket.

A lust for the feminine cavity,
Some chastise as willful depravity.
But surely the fact
That bodies attract
Is due not to sin, but to gravity.

Telegraphy became a hit.
It's first three notes dit-dah-dit.
If they'd dit-dit-dit-dah,
They would have gone far,
But Ludvig Van had copywrit.

Galileo said, "My inquest proves
That the Earth is the object that moves.
But THE INQUEST, alas,
Will fry my mortal ass
If the power in Rome disapproves."

This Earth with strange folk does abound,
Who think the Earth's flat and not round,

And it seems they cannot
Tell, I'm sure you know what,
From a hole which you find in the ground.

Beggs sampled the chef's treat Chinese--
Lee's sauce with two eggs, it did please.
"This angle," said Beggs,
"With two equal eggs,
I believe is a nice sauce o' Lee's."

An environmentalist, O'Boyle
Gave her kids Ex-lax and castor oil.
She wanted her brood
To return all the food,
Directly back to the soil.

Archimedes while dipped to his waist,
Tried screwing a mermaid in haste.
But he failed to account
For his weight in the mount,
Which equaled the water displaced.

A fat lady who called herself Sue
Hadn't bathed since the year '92.
She thought she'd an aura
Of fauna and flora;
She smelled like the St. Louis Zoo!

It pains me that girls with a brain
Will choose from rough sex to abstain;
What can give them displeasure
Is another man's treasure,
Like the spreader, the whip, and the chain!

There's a young Spanish girl named Donna
Who'd a most irritating persona.
She'd trouble and vex
The opposite sex

And promise to screw them manana.

Brother Borr said, "Indulgence and fun
I eschew," but cloaked truth in pun.
"I am sober, and choose
To abstain from all booze.
As for pleasures of sex, I have nun."

Far better than cure is prevention,
At least that was once the contention.
Though it does seem to me,
What with rife STD,
That prevention equates with abstention.

The Baptists can't hide their chagrin
Now that Disney treats roomies as kin.
So they boycott the house
Of the Anti-Christ mouse,
'Cause the mouse condones living in sin.

Disney OK'd the Gay Pride parades
Causing those Southern Baptist tirades.
"We'll shun the house
Of that Mickey Mouse,
And his goofy friends, the gay blades.

The young man's new penis dilator
Was bought with hope he could sate her.
But when tested in action,
Her dissatisfaction
Proved a serious satyr deflator!

Your Honor," said Ms. Paula Jones,
"On the pretense of answering his phones,
He asked me to watch
While he unzipped his crotch,
And he then tried to jump on my bones."

There was a young woman named Stacey
Who somehow endeavored to chase me.
She was right in her prime
And she fucked so divine,
That the ring on her finger escaped me.

A silver-tongued poet, quite oft
Lured a score of young girls to his loft.
First to visit the bard
No doubt found it hard,
But the rest, it is said, had it soft.

I enjoy making love to a dame
With a fine callipygian frame.
I'll admit if I must
To some lust for the bust,
But the feeling just isn't the same.

A construction worker thought it a howl,
To address women with language most foul.
Till a dyke on a bike
Took a dislike...
There's now a beer can in his bowel.

I abhor the onslaught of snow,
When the cold makes a man...well, you know,
Shrivel up like a raisin.
I find it amazin'
There exist any young Eskimo.

With delicious breasts she is graced--
Her nipples are honey to taste;
My wife's pair is small,
But I'm pleased after all,
'Cause more than a mouthful's a waste!

Kathy Gifford has been in a stew--
With her ex, she's have nothing to do!
So bid Ellen Degeneris,

Dreaming of her 'mons veneris'
"Kathy, can I be frank with you."

Growled Pa Bear, "Someone's been in my bed!"
"And mine," Ma said, "Look at that spread!"
Baby bear, most polite,
Gently put out the light.
"Nighty night, folks," was all that he said.

As a kid, when we rode on the bus,
Deep questions we'd often discuss:
"Would it come off divine,
Or just blow out her spine,
If Superman did it with Lois?"

That fellow who kept a dead whore
In his cave, I suppose on the floor:
True, he'd save lots of money,
But what good's a dead honey,
'Cause her blowjobs ain't shit anymore.

Thanksgiving, the Pilgrims' first feast,
In the frigid and nasty Northeast;
They were warmly dressed,
Though I would have guessed,
The Indians were wearing their least.

Twin sisters, named Coral and Carol,
Were laid out in their finest apparel.
Their life had been moral;
For Carol a chorale
Was sung, and for Coral, a carol.

My semi-demented Aunt Alice
Went to dine at the archbishop's Palace;
But she fell into sin,
Drinking far too much gin,
And pissed in his second-best chalice.

The Archbishop, surprised, said, "O daughter!
You have done what you shouldn't have oughter;
And in cases like this,
While we don't call it piss,
I'll be damned if it's quite 'Holy Water.'"

There once was a young man named Cass
Whose balls were made of spun glass
He'd clang them together
And play "Stormy Weather"
While lightning shot out of his ass

Oh! cabin boy, Oh! cabin boy,
You dirty little nipper
You lined your ass
With broken glass
And circumscised the skipper

There was a young lady named Ransom
Who was ravished three times in a hansom
When she cried out for more
A voice from the floor
Said "Lady I'm Simpson not Sampson!"

An Argentine gaucho named, Bruno
Said "There is one thing that I do Know"
"A woman is fine"
"And a sheep is divine"
"But a Llama is numero uno!"

There was a young lady of Kent
Who said that she knew what it meant
When men asked her to dine,
Gave her cocktails and wine:
She knew what it meant, but she went.

www.ingramcontent.com/pod-product-compliance
Lightning Source LLC
Chambersburg PA
CBHW051822090426
42736CB00011B/1609